I0829906

CORPORATE GOVERNANCE FOR SMALL AND MEDIUM-SIZED BUSINESSES IN AFRICAN ECONOMIES

Promoting the Appreciation and Adoption of Corporate Governance Principles for SMEs in Africa

DR. CHINYERE ALMONA

Foreword by Professor Mervyn E. King, SC.
Fmr. Chairman, King Committee on
Corporate Governance in South Africa

authorHOUSE®

AuthorHouse™
1663 Liberty Drive
Bloomington, IN 47403
www.authorhouse.com
Phone: 833-262-8899

Published by AuthorHouse 12/15/2020

ISBN: 978-1-7283-7316-4 (sc)
ISBN: 978-1-7283-7315-7 (e)

Library of Congress Control Number: 2020917346

Print information available on the last page.

Dedicated to the owners and managers of small and medium-sized businesses in the African region—for their passion, tenacity, and resilience in setting up and running businesses in such a difficult terrain.

I salute your vision and courage.

ENDORSEMENTS

Dr. Almona brings her considerable experience and undoubted expertise in corporate governance in Africa to bear in expanding on the benefits of good corporate governance practices that can be selectively applied to small and medium-sized enterprises. The growth of private sector businesses in economies dominated mainly by State-owned enterprises will depend on the formalization of Small and Medium-sized Enterprises and encouraging their contribution to sustainable economic growth. This is achieved not just through new and creative ideas for business opportunities, of which there are plenty in Africa, but the accompanying development of good business practices that will encourage trust in these enterprises and their ability to access capital that will facilitate their growth and formality. This book elegantly offers insights and practical guidance drawn from Dr. Almona's extensive experience and wisdom, which are both timely and opportune.

Philip Armstrong
Director of Governance, Gavi Alliance, Geneva, Switzerland.
Board Vice-Chair, International Corporate
Governance Network (ICGN)

Corporate Governance for Small and Medium-Sized Businesses in African Economies provides practical and relevant insights for entrepreneurs committed to attracting financing and building successful businesses. It will play a critical role in strengthening corporate governance structures in the African business landscape and ensuring that more businesses survive for generations.

Ndidi Okonkwo Nwuneli
Founder, LEAP Africa
Co-Founder, AACE Foods & Sahel Consulting

known that yesterday's SMEs are today's top companies not only here in Africa but all over the world. This book is therefore a must-read for all who believe that SMEs are and will continue to be the engines of growth in our economies.

Mr Japheth Katto
Corporate Governance Consultant
Chairman, Stanbic Bank Uganda Limited
Kampala, Uganda

This book addresses a very critical but often overlooked aspect of running a small business, especially in this part of the world, where SMEs are more preoccupied with surmounting the existential challenges of poor infrastructure and inconsistent government policies. The real-world solution as it relates to the adoption of corporate governance by SMEs is aptly captured by the statement - "small businesses across Africa differ in size, structure, and stage of maturity; the expectation for corporate governance adoption should, therefore, be in alignment with these characteristics." This approach is a welcome concept as it encourages small businesses to implement corporate governance practices best suited to their current stage of development, and from which they can identify and reap benefits in the short term—a stark contrast from the usual, one-size-fits-all approach commonly adopted in the past.

The author has done justice to this germane issue affecting SMEs. This book is timely, as many SMEs are currently reviewing and restructuring their operations in response to the COVID-19 pandemic and its effects on businesses. The book presents well-researched ideas in an easy-to-read and articulate manner. I would recommend this book to budding and established entrepreneurs as a guide to navigating the process of instituting corporate governance to create a sustainable business.

Shekarau Omar,
(Sadaukin Katagum),
Executive Director, Small and Medium Enterprises,
Bank of Industry, Nigeria.

It is truly an honor for me to give a review on this outstanding book written by a very formidable woman, Dr. Chinyere, who I met through the African Corporate Governance Network. The depth of her knowledge always amazed me, and it was my heartfelt wish that she would share this knowledge in a manner that could cascade in the African education systems and the world at large. This way, our world would have the best governance system and many sustainable businesses.

Here you go!

As a fellow African woman, and a proud Ethiopian, I feel that most African indigenous SMEs often phase-out as governance is the least important subject due to tight-knitted-family engagement in businesses. African companies are formed to bring solidarity among relatives. Usually, the concept of Corporate Governance is ignored as it may be considered a betrayal of family members if one wishes to make dismissal decisions to curb asset embezzlement. That is why we hardly find generational companies that exist beyond the 4th generation. The existing and the future generation must change the misconception, and this book shall be the <u>changemaker's manual.</u>

Thank you, Dr. Chinyere. You shall be remembered as one who changed the African CG history.

Tihitina Mulushewa Legesse (Lady T)
Managing Director at Waryt Furniture, Addis Ababa, Ethiopia
Member of the Board of Directors, Ethiopian
Institute of Corporate Governance

Corporate Governance for SMEs in African economies is a vital component in the fabric of the business environment, of which individual businesses are the strands. Corporate Governance goes far beyond being a system of control and into the long-term sustainability of the entity, ensuring it outlives the founder. There is a long list of very successful African businesses that start up, become economically viable, grow, and ensure the founder and immediate family enjoy a comfortable life. Only for the business to die along with the founder, or shortly thereafter. Running a business comes with many challenges; namely production, quality control, packaging, marketing, financial recording and control, the list is endless. Also of great importance are the 'people challenges,' termed Human Resources Management. When these include family relationships, it adds another dimension to the myriad challenges facing the company. Corporate

Governance is vital in the separation of various parameters (ownership/ management/personal/family…) which, when mixed, may become toxic.

This book is a welcome addition to resource materials that will be of great help to SME's in African Economies to move them forward into the future and ensure their sustainable viability.

Christopher Forster
Managing Director, Picton Services (SL) Ltd. Sierra Leone
President, Sierra Leone Chamber of Commerce, Industry and Agriculture

Congratulations on a wonderful piece of work! The depth and breadth of the content are so well suited to any SME that wants to run ethical, honorable, sustainable businesses, and so uplift the African economy. In an era where corruption seems to have become the unquestioned way of achieving business success, this book answers the question I have heard so many SME owners ask:
"So how can corporate governance help my business?"
This book proves that corporate governance is not too difficult or costly for SMEs to implement. All it takes is the commitment to run a properly governed business and an understanding of the driving force behind the principles and practices of good corporate governance.

Juanita Vorster
Certified Director, Entrepreneur, Business Advisor
Johannesburg, South Africa

As the head of an African SME that began as a family business and successfully transitioned into a publicly listed and traded corporation, I have experienced first-hand what a real transformation in corporate governance and commitment to the ongoing work of identifying and improving the gaps as the company develops and grows can do for a business. Dr. Chinyere Almona's comprehensive book is an invaluable and inspiring resource for leaders looking to undertake a similar transformation and move their companies to the next level.

Based on extensive research and years of experience in the field, this book takes on a broad and ambitious vision of positively impacting the overall business climate of emerging economies in Africa by strengthening SMEs, which are the continent's main engines of growth. It delivers on that vision by presenting a strong theoretical framework coupled with actionable guidelines and recommendations that are grounded in the reality of operating an SME in Africa and are adaptable to the stages of a business's development and its unique needs.

Abir Leheta
Chairman & CEO
Egytrans, Egypt

No such thing as coincidence in business.
Dr. Almona's work was mentioned to me as I was, and still am, experiencing every imaginable challenge to running a business in an African country. I have been running what could be categorized as an SME for the past ten years. And every single parameter in my business environment reminds me of how vital Corporate Governance is.
First, defining an SME versus a large corporation was challenging, particularly in my Western Francophone country. Then, running a family business has its corporate governance challenges and load of burdens. Today, as the business grows larger, seeking and engaging new partners, shareholders, and investors, there are higher governance expectations. I believe that will be the challenge for the next ten years, and this book provides the needed guidance.

Ismael BARMOU
Directeur général chez Société de Transformation Alimentaire (STA sa)
Republic of the Niger

Dr. Almona's book, Corporate Governance for Small and Medium-sized Businesses in African Economies, contains a wealth of information on Corporate Governance directed towards small entrepreneurs.

Dr. Almona's approach is extremely logical and the concepts expressed are easy to follow. The book is very much a corporate governance user handbook and should be a great help to African entrepreneurs in making their businesses sustainable over time.

Tim Taylor
Chairman
Scott & Co Ltd
Riche Terre, Mauritius

The arrival of a publication on the governance of African SMEs indicates the importance of the subject in the economy of this continent. This book, or rather this working tool, is timely to accompany African companies engaged in the battle of diversification and competitiveness through generous upgrade programs, highlighting the benefits of rigorous management as a "good father." At a time when, across the continent, the informal sector is growing faster than the African economy, where governments and employers are struggling to convince economic actors of the merits of good corporate governance, one can only welcome such an educational tool that is accessible to everyone.

African SMEs no longer evolve in a closed universe; they evolve in an ecosystem within which they interact to the best of their interests, making good governance a prerequisite for a serene relationship with stakeholders. The author of this book has spared no effort to offer the reader as comprehensive a picture as possible of the company, its operations, and its governance. The future of Africa depends on this social responsibility that must be assumed by all business leaders in the first place as producers of wealth and providers of jobs.

Best wishes of success to the author

Mr. Slim Othmani
President of the Think-tank CARE
Chairman of NCA Rouiba, and founder of Hawkama el Djazaïr
Algiers, Algeria

Lack of organization and the absence of good corporate governance remain a challenge for SMEs in Africa. On a continent where SMEs account for 90 % of all businesses, there is an urgent need to raise more awareness of this situation. Once addressed, it will enable sustainable growth for our emerging economies.

Dr. Almona's book highlights what African companies need to know in terms of ethical rules and appropriated values for their businesses' effective management.

Dr. Edoh Kossi Amenounve,
Chief Executive Officer
BRVM - Bourse Régionale des Valeurs Mobilières
Abidjan, Côte D'ivoire

CONTENTS

ACKNOWLEDGMENTS

I am grateful to God for the inspiration to write a book in a different genre from my first four books.

Appreciation is owed to my family: to my husband, Pastor Obi Almona, for being a pillar of support; to my children, Chidumebi, Ginikachukwu, and Chukwudiebube, for giving me space when I needed it; to my parents, Rev. (Canon) I. A. Nwankwo and Professor (Mrs.) J. N. Nwankwo, both of blessed memory, for building the foundation of my scholarly curiosity.

I am indebted to my colleagues at the International Finance Corporation and specifically the Africa Corporate Governance Program team, under the leadership of Dr. Roman Zyla, for walking by me in the adventure across sub-Saharan Africa. Creating corporate governance solutions for the past eight years has been a joyful challenge, and you all made it worthwhile. I am also thankful for all our clients and partners who adopted new ways of working to promote better corporate governance in the region.

I would like to thank my doctoral supervisor, Professor Jan A. Jurriëns, for his guidance and encouragement during my research on *Corporate Governance and Small and Medium-Sized Businesses in West Africa,* which is the basis of this book. His explicit and hard-hitting comments during the research were critical in shaping the outcome of my thesis. I also acknowledge the dean of Business School Netherlands, Marcel van Der Ham, under whose leadership I completed my doctoral program.

I am thankful to Prof Mervyn E. King, who graciously agreed to write the foreword for this book, buttressing the importance of corporate governance for SMEs. I am also grateful to Mrs. Ansie Ramalho, for facilitating the connection. Professor Gabriel Eweje of Massey Business School, Massey University, New Zealand, was very helpful. His accessible way of introducing and discussing complex subjects helped focus the process and provided the motivation to keep going. I would like to thank Mr. IK Mbagwu. Founder and CEO of Cumbrian Consult Ltd, Lagos, Nigeria, for taking the time to review the manuscript and make valuable technical input.

Finally, several other people in different parts of the world who are not mentioned here also encouraged and made contributions to this book. I thank all of them. My journey of a thousand miles started with a dream, supported by the encouragement of these good people, and it is ending with the beginning of new things.

FOREWORD

A company is an incapacitated artificial person. It has no heart, mind, or conscience of its own. The conscience of a company depends on whether its corporate leaders, the board of directors, are practicing conscious leadership.

It is irrelevant whether the business of the company is a small, medium, or large one. The principle that the directors are the conscience of the company is the same for all three types, as is the principle that they must make decisions in the long-term best interests of the health of the company and not any particular stakeholder or stakeholders.

In this book on corporate governance for SMEs, the various governance theories are discussed. Directors must be aware that the company is absolutely dependent on them and the management appointed by the directors to carry on the business of the company. The directors give the strategic direction decided on by the board, and management implements these decisions.

This book will be a helpful guide to all directors of small- and medium-sized companies, as the book sets out the basics of corporate governance. Directors must also be aware that the decisions the board makes have outcomes and that the company must achieve those outcomes: value creation in a sustainable manner; adequate and effective controls with informed oversight; trust and confidence by the community in the company in which it operates, with legitimacy of operations and with an ethical culture and effective leadership.

In this time of economic and viral crises, directors have to have an integrated, collaborative and compromising mindset in an endeavour to ensure that a company survives these crises. Hence, I have coined the word *coronanomics* to describe these two crises in which large and small companies are swimming. The relationship between the company and its stakeholders are critical in the context of coronanomics. There should be an agenda item at each board meeting of stakeholder relationships that will give the board a more informed oversight over management's proposals.

Sustainable Development Goal 17 provides for collaboration to achieve the other sixteen goals. The various restrictions that have been placed by governments to stem the spread of the coronavirus have resulted in poor economies becoming poorer. Directors, individually and collectively, must endeavor to ensure the survival of the company. If the nucleus of the company can survive, it will be easier to build it when the economy once again starts thriving in the next few years. If not, infrastructures will be sold at knockdown prices, and human capital will be dispersed, which will make it very difficult to resurrect that company.

This book is a useful guide for SMEs, who sometimes do not see the necessity to have outside, independent nonexecutive directors to help the board make more informed judgment calls in the best long-term interests of the health of the company.

Prof Mervyn E. King, SC
Fmr. Chairman, King Committee on Corporate Governance in South Africa
https://www.mervynking.co.za/pages/profile.htm

PREFACE

A few months ago, I visited a classmate whom I have not seen since we left high school (grade twelve) over thirty years ago. We chatted about life, family career, hobbies, and things that have happened in our lives over the years.

She shared that she recently started a small business in the fashion industry in Lagos, Nigeria. Excitedly, she described how she had ventured into the business, what her vision for the company was, and some thoughts on how to move the business beyond its infancy stage. As the conversation progressed, she asked what I did at my place of work. I explained that I advise companies and corporate boards on how to adopt good corporate governance practices that will help their businesses be better governed and managed. This seemed too broad - she wanted specifics of what my work entailed. So I explained that I currently lead a team that supports corporate governance improvements across sub-Saharan Africa by moving several levers of change, including developing policies, building capacity/expertise, and creating awareness of the importance of good corporate governance.

At some point in the discussion, she asked what my doctorate topic was. I told her that the focus was to help SMEs address the challenges of adopting good corporate governance practices. She thought about it for a while, and I perceived she was adding up my work responsibilities as a corporate governance professional, my doctoral passion for SMEs, and her need for some form of support. She eyed me coyly and asked, "So how can you help my business?" Before I could think up a reasonable response, she quickly added, "Is my business too small for such (*i.e.,* *corporate governance*)?"

I explained to her that corporate governance is relevant for all businesses, regardless of size, complexity, or sector. The adoption of corporate governance to any business will depend on what the business owner wants to achieve. I then asked her how successful she wanted her business to be, and she quipped, "Very successful." Her eyes lit up, and she appeared to have been transported to a future day and time when her business is booming, profits are rising, and customers are beating a path to her doorstep.

I beckoned her back to the present and asked her if anything was preventing her business from attaining the heights she had dreamed of. She thought about my question for a while and mentioned a few factors, including the location of her store and access to funds for expansion. This was an excellent start; so I asked her how she currently manages her cash inflows and outflows. She confided that she sometimes spends cash received from customers on domestic exigencies.

I probed further, asking about her staff, trying to figure out who plays what role within the business. It became apparent that she played multiple roles—chief executive officer, chief operations officer, risk manager, accountant, human resources officer, customer service, secretary, and so on. All the other employees are in production. In fact, my friend singlehandedly controls every aspect of her business, developing the business strategies and systems on the go, making all decisions, and doing whatever is required to meet customer demands. Understandably, most entrepreneurs are willing to take in a broader range of responsibilities during the startup phase, as founders often wear many hats.

My friend's business is best described as a microenterprise in its nascent stage; however, her story and circumstances are like that of a typical small business in Africa. I shared with her certain corporate governance principles contained in this book. She left our mini-reunion with some specific actions that she needed to take. These included keeping better records, separating business and personal cash flows, establishing a salary for herself, and committing to living within the means of her salary regardless of expected challenges or family expectations.

Imbibing an appropriate level of governance at an early stage of a small business is beneficial. Helping SMEs appreciate the positive effect of governance on the company, and simplifying what needs to be done, will enable them to embrace the concept and enhance the ease of adoption.

INTRODUCTION

The term "Corporate governance" tends to invoke a perception that it is relevant only to large corporations and, therefore, not on the minds of most small-business owners and managers in African economies. Yet, most of the issues on the mind of the owner of a typical African SME, such as customers, funding, market share/penetration, operations, growth, and expansion, can be addressed if appropriate corporate governance practices are adopted.

Corporate governance is the system by which a company is directed and controlled; and the arrangement of the separation of ownership and management. A well-organized separation ensures that there is no tension between the interests of the business owner(s) and those of the managers. To business owner(s), therefore, sound corporate governance is a central tenet to the protection of their interests and the achievement of optimal business performance.

It is often stated that SMEs are the engine of development because they play a vital role in job creation from the grassroots, innovation, and long-term economic development. Unfortunately, only a small fraction of African SMEs succeeds in achieving exceptional performance, sustainable growth, and effective succession. Clearly, there is a gap in establishing practical and sustainable ways to increase the size of that fraction and get African SMEs to move beyond the founder's lifetime.

Growth and Development in Africa

In my work across Africa, leading the IFC Africa Corporate Governance Advisory team, I have often wondered why Africa's growth and development have been prolonged even though there is enormous potential to be a great continent. Africa is richly endowed with both natural and human resources and is among the wealthiest regions, but the continent is almost as economically weak as it was two decades ago.

The rate of GDP growth lags far behind those of other regions of the developing world; the levels of investment are also relatively low. A reason for the low investment levels and lack of access to finance is in part because of the perceived risk of doing business in Africa due to poor governance. It is clear to me that growth in Africa will not occur until some essential elements of development are put in place. One of these elements is broad access to finance for entrepreneurs (SMEs), which will strengthen the capacity of the private sector. In the absence of this, the private sector will not be able to attract or utilize capital to generate employment and economic growth.

Over the years, my team initiated various corporate governance reforms in the African region, such as development and revision of corporate governance regulations, capacity building, establishing governance courses in major universities, and developing corporate governance frameworks for SMEs. These are all geared toward ensuring that there is sufficient capacity on the continent to address issues of corporate governance systematically.

Governing Small Businesses

For SMEs to continue to play a vital role in job creation and economic development, businesses must be successful, stable, and sustainable. Unfortunately, several small businesses are endangered. Owners and managers of SMEs are struggling to obtain finance and, in some cases, are unable to do so because they do not have the structures that banks (and other potential financiers and investors) require. Some small businesses grow and then decline very rapidly at the demise of the founder. Hence, it would be great if good corporate governance were demystified, and the related principles and practices were described in ways that small businesses could relate to. This would make the adoption of good corporate governance practices attainable for small businesses.

Good corporate governance also benefits the economy and broader society as a whole. According to the Organisation for Economic

Co-operation and Development (OECD), "the presence of an effective corporate governance system, within an individual company and across the economy as a whole, helps to provide a degree of confidence that is necessary for the proper functioning of a market economy."

Many SMEs do not sufficiently understand and appreciate the benefits of good corporate governance; nor the fact that poor governance can jeopardize their dream of a great business initiative. As an African, I want to see growth and stability in the African continent. My desire to understand the challenges that small businesses face in adopting corporate governance, and my search for ways to ameliorate the burden, came about as I contemplated the potential positive economic effect of having well-run SMEs in Africa.

Various research studies conducted in the last two decades indicate that suitable corporate governance structures bring many positive outcomes to companies. These benefits include access to external funding for growth and expansion, access to more extensive networks, and better decision-making. Despite these benefits, SMEs continue to struggle with adopting good corporate governance practices. It appears, therefore, that the challenges of adopting good corporate governance practices outweigh the benefits for these small companies. The primary reasons that have been given by a lot of SMEs for not establishing corporate governance structures include concern about suitability and the feeling that involving others in the running of the business or extensive disclosure of business information means letting go of control or losing autonomy.

To say that good *corporate governance* contributes significantly to a successful establishment is an obvious conclusion. However, small businesses across Africa differ in size, structure, and stage of maturity; the expectation for corporate governance adoption should, therefore, be in alignment with these varying characteristics. An understanding of this heterogeneity in the SME sector is essential in discussing an appropriate set of corporate governance practices.

In a Nutshell: A Quick Overview

The viewpoints, principles, and ideas contained in this book are presented in three separate but interconnected sections.

Section one sets the scene, providing an overview of the tenets of corporate governance from theoretical and practical perspectives. This overview establishes the foundational context upon which the book rests. The starting point is the exploration of various definitions and descriptions of corporate governance and their possible implications. A discussion of the philosophies provides a connection between the theories and practices of corporate governance that are relevant to SMEs. Further, a detailed review of the elements of sound corporate governance contributes to the understanding of how to develop an effective corporate governance system. The relationship between the practice of good corporate governance and company performance is explored from the perspective of previous research studies and practical experience.

The second section of the book offers insights into the world of SMEs. It presents the importance of SMEs as the heartbeat of job creation and the engine of economic development in Africa. The section further highlights the five lifecycle stages of an SME, each with its own set of challenges, and the related corporate governance structures that can be adopted. The perceived dichotomy between the concept of corporate governance and how an SME is governed was debunked by reviewing the various reasons that SMEs fail and endorsing the fact that corporate governance is not a one-size-fits-all concept. The desire of African entrepreneurs to have an enduring business and the contribution of corporate governance to success and sustainability make it clear that corporate governance for SMEs is not an oxymoron.

In the third and final section of this book, I share some frameworks and supporting ideas, including the views of key stakeholders on the implications of corporate governance for SME. In this regard, the views of stakeholders on corporate governance and how it contributes to and promotes SMEs' business performance, stability, and sustainability are highlighted. The novel Five-Way Directional model© is revealed, as well as the seven business capitals, which SMEs can rely upon for business success. Understanding and exploring the dynamics of the seven capitals can help SMEs to improve business practices, engage better with stakeholders, and ensure business growth with a positive impact. The final piece is a consideration for the governance of family businesses, providing insight on the effect of family ownership on SME governance.

Vision for the Book and Intended Purpose

This book will unveil practical ways that corporate governance can support an SME's quest for long-term growth, competitiveness, and sustainability. Its focus will be on demystifying corporate governance and providing relatable perspectives of small business governance. This will be done by aligning the stages of business growth and the forms of corporate governance that contribute value to the business. An essential addition would be a foray into what needs to be done to improve the adoption of corporate governance by SME owners/managers, regulators, and investors.

I hope that this book will make a tangible impact on the dynamics of the overall discussion around SMEs and corporate governance in Africa. While I believe that it will set the stage for greater exploration and discovery, it will also help in changing the business climate. Improving the business climate will occur if this book enables a more unambiguous expression by SMEs and their stakeholders of what corporate governance means, how much value it can add, and how to adopt it effectively. It is therefore, a very practical guide to the implementation of effective governance for SMEs in Africa.

This book is also the foundation for my vision to develop and facilitate growth programs for African SMEs. The growth program will provide ongoing practical guidance on how to implement critical elements of corporate governance that will enable long-term growth, business expansion, and financial stability. The ultimate goal is to enhance the adoption of corporate governance principles and practices by SMEs in African economies.

SECTION ONE
TENETS OF CORPORATE GOVERNANCE

CHAPTER 1

ABOUT CORPORATE GOVERNANCE

Defining Corporate Governance

There is no single universally accepted definition or description of the concept of corporate governance. Several definitions have been put forward by different practitioners depending on the discipline, situation, or context in which it is being used.

Corporate governance is basically a set of relationships between a company's board, management, shareholders, and society, within an institutional framework. These relationships evolve into the corporate governance framework, which is "the system by which companies are directed and controlled," according to the well-known Sir Adrian Cadbury report. Another scholar indicated that, "Corporate governance is concerned with the processes, systems, practices and procedures as well as the formal and informal rules that govern institutions, the manner in which these rules and regulations are applied and followed, the relationships that these rules and regulations determine or create, and the nature of those relationships."[1] In the *King II Report* Mervyn King described corporate governance as being "essentially about leadership.

… Leadership for efficiency in order for companies to compete effectively in the global economy, and thereby create jobs;

… Leadership for probity because investors require confidence and assurance that the management of a company will behave honestly and with integrity in regard to their

... shareholders and others;

... Leadership with responsibility as companies are increasingly called upon to address legitimate social concerns relating to their activities; and,

... Leadership that is both transparent and accountable because otherwise business leaders cannot be trusted, and this will lead to the decline of companies and the ultimate demise of a country's economy."[2]

Corporate governance is defined in the *King IV* report as the exercise of ethical and effective leadership by the governing body towards the achievement of an ethical culture, good performance, effective control and legitimacy[3]. There also exists a simple idea that governance exists to translate the wishes of an organization's owner(s) into performance for the organization.

In another context, Sir Adrian Cadbury described corporate governance as a framework to encourage the efficient use of resources and equally to require accountability for the stewardship of those resources, with an aim to align as nearly as possible the interests of individuals, corporations and the society.[4] The wide range of definitions available reflects the different perspectives and priorities of the stakeholders involved in the corporate governance discussions. Further, the definition could depend on whether it is in the context of large public firms or small and medium enterprises.

The term "governance" is an English derivative of a Latin word "*gubernāre*," or the ancient Greek word "*Kubernetes*," both of which can be translated literarily to mean "steer, be at the helm of; govern, rule, command, direct." In this sense, therefore, governance could be presented as a process of steering or providing direction to an institution.

There is also a parallel description of governance as *cybernetic*, a description that aligns it with an ancient Greek word *kybernetikos*, meaning "good at steering." Cybernetics, according to its original application in mathematics, refers to "the feedback and control mechanism by which a system, and any system for that matter, keeps itself oriented towards the goals for which it was created."[5] The combination of "giving direction" and maintaining control" are two sides of the governance coin. Corporate governance seeks to solve a fundamental problem for anyone charged with giving direction to a company by establishing how business owners/ directors/managers can drive the company forward while keeping it under prudent control.

The need for corporate governance is considered to have arisen because of the separation of management and ownership in organizations. This points somewhat to the shareholder view. However, any definition of corporate governance that focuses only on shareholders and the relationship between them and the management is considered limited or a narrow perspective.[6] A straightforward description of corporate governance is having the right people in the right positions making the right decisions and taking the right actions all the time.

Considering the diversity and variety of definitions that exist, it would be necessary to adopt a working definition that would be both relevant and applicable to SMEs. My preference would be the broad definition from the Cadbury Report, which states, "Corporate Governance is the system by which companies are directed and controlled." My reason for this is that the definition does not specifically mention boards of directors or relationships with stakeholders, which may or may not be applicable to SMEs. It focuses on the "direction" and "control" of companies. Then, drawing from another definition which explicitly indicates the purpose that a corporate governance system should achieve, I would add to Cadbury's definition, the purpose or focus of directing and controlling the business, which is the profitability and long-term growth of the enterprise.

The resultant contextual definition of corporate governance is "a system by which companies are directed and controlled to enable profitability and long-term growth of the enterprise." Adopting good corporate governance standards and practices is important to every organization, regardless of size, and should be encouraged for the interests of the investors and other stakeholders.

Rising Interest in Corporate Governance

Corporate governance has been the subject of discussion as a result of incidences of corporate fraud, accounting scandals, misleading disclosures, excessive compensation packages, insider trading, self-dealing, and possible civil and criminal liabilities of corporate leaders and organizations.

Accordingly, these have alerted both internal and external stakeholders to intensify their scrutiny of the soundness of corporate governance practices within companies.[7]

Indeed, lack of sound governance practices was regarded as the major contributory factor to past financial crises as further described below. In reference to these financial crises, there were indications that some institutions were regarded prior to the financial crisis as being too big to fail.[8] Eventually, it was revealed that they lacked good corporate governance practices, leading to the financial crisis. It would appear, therefore, that when companies fail, they do so mainly because of corporate governance lapses.

Corporate governance as a subject matter has gained increased visibility and exploration today when compared with two decades ago. The increasing interest in corporate governance is largely a result of the increasing prevalence of corporate scandals and the impact of corporate failure on the economy. On the flip side of each scandal is the awareness of the benefit that good corporate governance practices can add to business performance.

Importantly, the concept of corporate governance which originated as a concept focused on the shareholders (as providers of business capital), has broadened to incorporate all stakeholders of a business.[9] There are now increased concerns and activism about institutions' environmental and social (or sustainability) footprints over the last decades.[10] Corporate sustainability is commonly understood as a company's ability to positively influence environmental, social, and economic developments through their governance practices and market presence and to manage that influence appropriately.[11] I have discovered that companies practicing better corporate governance also have better environmental and social (E&S) practices. The sustainability perspective requires companies to engage strategically with key stakeholders to guarantee the company's long-term survival,[12] and successful successions.

Another aspect of corporate governance deals with improving decision-making to maximize the long-term objectives of the company. In this case, a sound governance approach should result in better decisions for SMEs, thus enhancing its strategic competitive position. I have also discovered from practical personal experience that SMEs in Africa are constantly seeking finance to grow or expand their business ventures, therefore adopting appropriate corporate governance structures should place them in good stead with potential financiers. This factor was supported by Ghanaian researchers, who allude to the fact that SMEs in Ghana have better access to finance with the adoption of good governance systems.[13] Indeed, corporate governance has the potential to make companies more attractive to potential investors and financiers.

The Importance of Corporate Governance

Academics and professionals have been paying great attention to how corporate governance practices influence the strategies and performance of management; and ultimately affecting organizational growth and sustainability. Evidence from various sources[14] suggests that adopting good corporate governance practices increases investors' trust, thereby generating appropriate goodwill. Other benefits include,

- … Increase in a company's valuation, making it attractive to investors.
- … Increased access to financing;
- … lower cost of capital due to perceived lower risk;
- … better performance due to better decision-making; and
- … improvement in the treatment of stakeholders, such as employees, suppliers, and customers.

There is a correlation between good corporate governance practices and investors' interest in a company. I find, from personal dealings with investors, that when good corporate governance practices exist within an organization, investors' perception of risks is diminished. Companies with better corporate governance attract a better average credit risk rating by almost 1.50 points. Consequently, good corporate governance has significant implications for the growth prospects of a business and by implication, a nation's economy.

More recently, there has been a lot of focus on establishing a correlation between corporate governance and the economic performance of a businesses. This has culminated in the development of the business case for corporate governance. However, *correlation does not imply causation*, which means that a cause-and-effect relationship between corporate governance activities and quantitative business outcomes has not been unequivocally established.

Although causation proves elusive, there are safe indicators that suggest a strong linkage (correlation). Many writers have identified that good corporate governance practice has a positive influence on corporate performance and that companies with poor governance practices tend to be "less profitable, have more bankruptcy risks, lower valuations and pay out less to their shareholders."[15] In review a portfolio of investee companies, an investor discovered that companies that improved corporate governance practices during the investment period achieved about twenty percent higher performance.

The impact of poor corporate governance on institutions, governments, economies, and the society is also exhibited in the number of corporate scandals such as those associated with Enron, Volkswagen, Lehman Brothers, and many others. The Enron scandal has been adjudged to be undoubtedly one of the most famous corporate scandals of all time. Ineffective board leadership and lack of good corporate governance practices were at the root of the Enron's collapse as well as all other reported corporate scandals.

In describing the 1997 Asian currency crisis, it was reported that the crisis was exacerbated by weak corporate governance in the companies.[16] The 2007-2009 global crisis was also reported to have been caused by corporate governance failures. The financial institutions that were tagged too big to fail, apparently lacked discipline and accountability (effective corporate governance) leading to the financial crisis. The global financial crisis resulted in a massive "loss of economic output and financial wealth, psychological consequences and skill atrophy from extended unemployment."[17] Other outcomes included a significant increase in government and regulatory intervention in businesses and the associated costs of implementation. The scale of the crisis was unprecedented, and it was a huge shock (traumatic) to the financial system.[18] These cases and their humongous impact lend credence to the assertion that corporate governance is vital to companies' performances and to the general economy.

Considering the dearth of hard facts (quantitative evidence) most analyses of the business case for corporate governance have focused on qualitative rather than quantitative relationships, as arguments exist that indicate that weak corporate governance not only leads to poor firm performance and risky financing patterns but is also conducive to macroeconomic crises. Sadly, causation has always been difficult to prove, as there are various other factors that, when juxtaposed with poor governance, lead to failure.

While most elements of the business case for corporate governance derive from listed companies, there are elements that can be applied to any company regardless of its size. For example, extracting from the suggestion by a researcher[19] on the benefits of better corporate governance frameworks, SMEs can relate to *greater access to finance* and *improved performance*. The need for capital and better performance is a common factor between large companies and small companies.

In more recent times, effort is being made to quantify the benefits of good corporate governance, in order to show that there is a correlation between corporate governance structures and practices, and the performance of companies.[20] One of the overarching philosophies of the concept of corporate governance is to enable the maximization of the contribution of companies to the economy.[21] This is done through the establishment of appropriate checks-and-balances systems for the direction and control of the institution in a way that adds value to the company, its stakeholders, and the economy. To the extent that corporate governance can add a measure of value to a company—whether large, medium, or small—it is important to emphasize its relevance or appropriateness to small and medium-sized companies in Africa.

Historical Account of Corporate Governance Failure

The earliest account of corporate governance failure that I found is the case of Medici Bank[22], which started as a small business, grew quickly, without a robust corporate governance foundation, and declined just as fast as it grew. Medici Bank was founded by the Medici family, led by Giovanni di Bicci de' Medici. Medici Bank was a financial institution in Italy during the 15th century (1397–1494) and was the largest and most respected bank in Europe during its prime. There are some estimates that the Medici family was, for a period, the wealthiest family in Europe, owning art, land,

and gold. With this monetary wealth, the family acquired political power initially in Florence, and later in the broader spheres of Italy and Europe.

At one point, the Medicis managed most of the great fortunes in the European world, from members of royalty to merchants. There was even a time when the currency issued by the Medicis, *the florin*, was accepted and used throughout Europe as the preferred currency to conduct business, commerce, and trade.

An interesting fact to note is that one of Medici Bank's contribution to the professions of banking and accounting was the improvement of the general ledger system (which they pioneered), through the development of the double-entry system of tracking debits and credits or deposits and withdrawals. Since the Medicis were not only bankers but innovators in financial accounting, one would expect better corporate governance practices.

An early sign of the governance challenges of Medici Bank, was the near failure of one of its branches because of its manager's inclination to bribery and being overly motivated by money. Another branch got into trouble for much the same reason, in addition to series of risky lending practices that generated substantial non-performing loans. There were also other improper governance practices, such as related party transactions, poor hiring decisions, poor oversight, lack of accountability and weak operational control. Another misjudgment or failure by the owners of Medici Bank was placing operational trust in a not-too qualified family member instead of in more trustworthy professional managers. There were a few fraudulent activities too, as the bank stacked up substantial non-business-related expenses due to the family's profligate spending, extravagant lifestyle, and failure to control the managers, leading eventually to insolvency.

As far back as the Medici Bank case occurred, the lapses described above continue to exist in current cases of failed companies. Reading through the list of corporate failures in Africa, which has mostly South African entities, it appears to mirror the Medic Bank case. This trend suggests that business owners and leaders have not learned much from the failures of the past. Secondly, the trend emphasizes the importance of the adoption of good corporate governance regardless of the size of the business.

Chapter Summary: Points to Pause and Ponder

- Corporate governance has no universally accepted definition or description. However, Sir Adrian Cadbury 1992 report's definition is widely in use. The report defines corporate governance as the system by which companies are directed and controlled.
- Corporate governance is not a one-size-fits-all concept, but it is contextual and applicable to all sizes of business.
- The business case for corporate governance is typically more qualitative than quantitative. There is more reference to a correlation effect than a causation effect.
- Corporate governance deals with improving decision-making in order to maximize the long-term objectives of the company. Therefore, a sound governance approach results in better decisions for SMEs, thus enhancing its strategic competitive position.
- Corporate governance is a significant factor in improving economic efficiency and growth. It has been empirically tested that a company's good governance practices give a positive signal to investors.
- Corporate governance has been of increasing interest around the world as there is mounting evidence that good practices and standards in corporate governance bring growth and increase sustainability and returns in a company.
- Good corporate governance is likely to reduce the cost of capital, encourage more stable sources of financing, and facilitate the broadening and deepening of local markets.
- Investing time and resources in improving corporate governance is positively associated with higher financial and economic returns
- It is expected that poverty alleviation and equitable distribution of wealth can be achieved in Africa by encouraging long-term economic growth through a well-planned and well-implemented approach to corporate governance.

CHAPTER 2

CORPORATE GOVERNANCE PHILOSOPHIES

There is a need to look at the evolution and varying theories in the field of corporate governance. This helps to shape the articulation of corporate governance concepts. The theoretical framework also provides a way to understand the nature and scope of corporate governance and its implications for small businesses. Corporate governance researchers view the corporate governance construct through the lens of a diverse set of theoretical perspectives to enhance understanding.[23]

The foremost theory in corporate governance is the agency theory, which was expanded into stewardship theory (to promote the goal of agency).[24] This evolved into the stakeholder theory (to make corporate governance attend to the needs of other stakeholder groups), and over time, there was a move towards the resource dependency theory. These were the core theories of corporate governance and considered the foundational tenets of the concept.

Agency Theory

Issues of corporate governance conceptually arise from the role of agency; therefore, agency theory is the preeminent theoretical lens.[25] Agency refers to the transfer of capital from the shareowners to the control of managers. The shareowners, through the board, delegate authority to management and entrust the board to act on their behalf. This separation of the ownership and control functions within a company inevitably leads to the managers being made responsible for the spending of *other people's money* (business capital).[26] For an effective relationship to be maintained between the providers of capital and company managers, high levels of trust must exist between both. The board is expected to monitor activities and decisions of management, therefore serving as the conduit between the two parties to ensure that the interests of the shareholders are fulfilled. Agency theory gives a good description of what the role and characteristics of the board of directors should entail.[27]

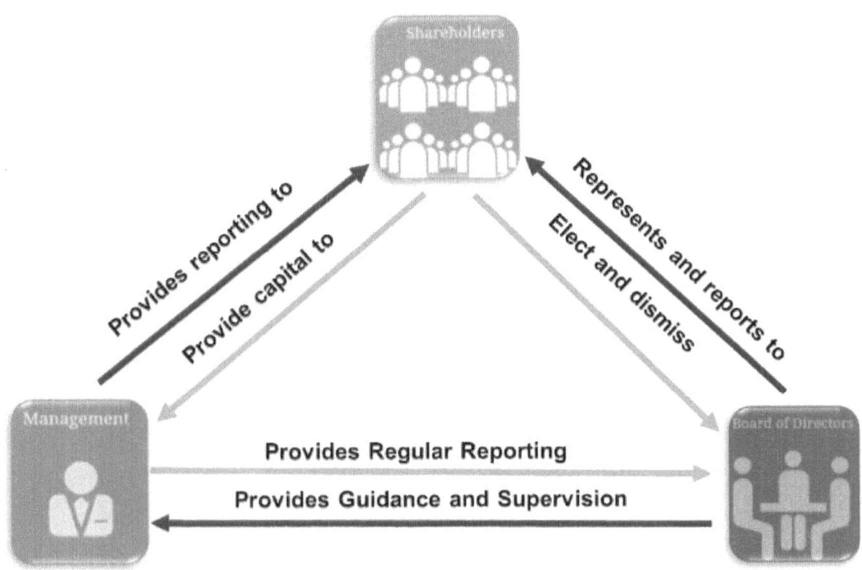

Figure 1 - Key Corporate Governance Players.

The inherent potential for conflicts of interest is a result of the separation of ownership and control in a company, because there is an assumption that the interest of the principal and the agent diverge; therefore, the theory emphasizes the monitoring responsibility of the board.[28] Monitoring by the board of management's activities is imperative because there are potential costs to the company if management is allowed to pursue its own interests at the expense of shareholders' interests.[29] However, the separation of ownership and control does not appear to be the case in a lot of SMEs.[30]

It has been suggested that agency theory provides a robust framework and a reference for studying some characteristics of owner-managed businesses.[31] However, based on my experience, while the agency theory provides a good backbone for the discussion of corporate governance as a concept, it does not address the needs and situations of most SMEs, where the shareholder (entrepreneur, owner of the business) is the manager (executive, managing director, chief executive officer) and also a member of the board (where a board exists). In this instance, the triangle above collapses, and the boxes come together.

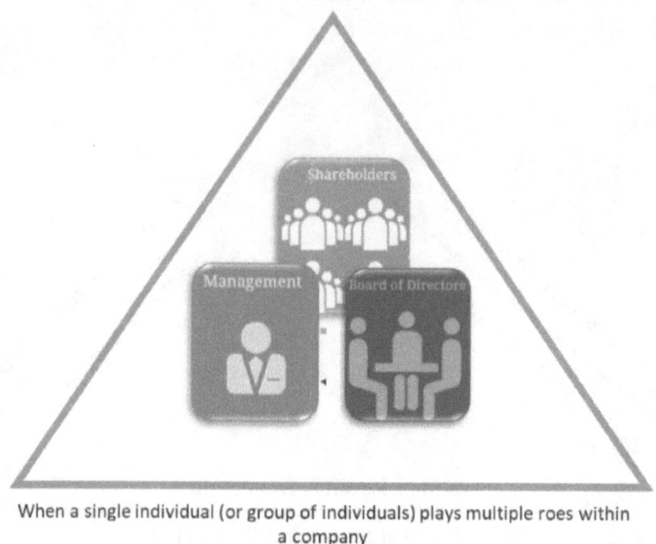

When a single individual (or group of individuals) plays multiple roes within a company

Figure 2 - When an individual plays all three roles

Stewardship Theory

Stewardship refers to the directors' role as guardians of the company's assets. Stewardship theory describes the agents (managers and employees) as stewards who should be able to align their motives with the objectives of the organization (and the principal) and therefore not be motivated by individual goals.[32] This behavior or attitude of the agents as stewards is typically due to various conditions, such as intrinsic personal features, needs, and motivations; identification with the company and commitment to company values; and a participative and trust-oriented management philosophy.[33] Further, the stewardship of the agent, who may be a board director or management, is focused on enhancing the company's performance, which, in the long run, benefits the principals (or shareholders). Therefore, stewardship theory and the values and behaviors of the agent are considered beneficial to owner-managed SMEs in the long run.[34]

Although the stewardship roles may appear more relevant when a company's owners (e.g., the shareowners) are different from its managers (which is not always the case with SMEs), researchers have suggested that stewardship theory provides a good basis for discussing governance within the context of owner-managed businesses,[35] as the managers and employees are *stewards* focused on the goals of the company. In small family businesses, family shareholders and family top executives are likely to act as stewards and to identify themselves strongly with the goals of the company. They view the company as an extension of themselves and thus regard the continuing health of the business as connected to their own personal well-being.

Stakeholder Theory

The stakeholder theory considers a company as an entity that is a sum total of its stakeholders and therefore having the responsibility to address the interests of the stakeholders rather than merely attend to the interests of shareholders.[36] Stakeholders of a company can be described as groups or individuals who contribute (voluntarily or involuntarily) to the business activities or operations; therefore, they affect the company and are affected by the company.[37] A broad definition of stakeholders would include regulators, employees, suppliers, customers, and the community.

Stakeholder theory provides a suitable theoretical lens for understanding corporate matters from the perspective of the value that the company's stakeholders seek or are interested in, and it helps understand how companies can develop governance mechanisms to deal with these. A stakeholder perspective is important from a governance point of view because managers tend to focus attention on measurable tasks that result in higher (profitable) performance.[38] Therefore, this enables managers to align their interests with those of the stakeholders, who presumably create value for the company. However, the challenge is in integrating the interests, expectations, and/or demands of the stakeholders of the company.

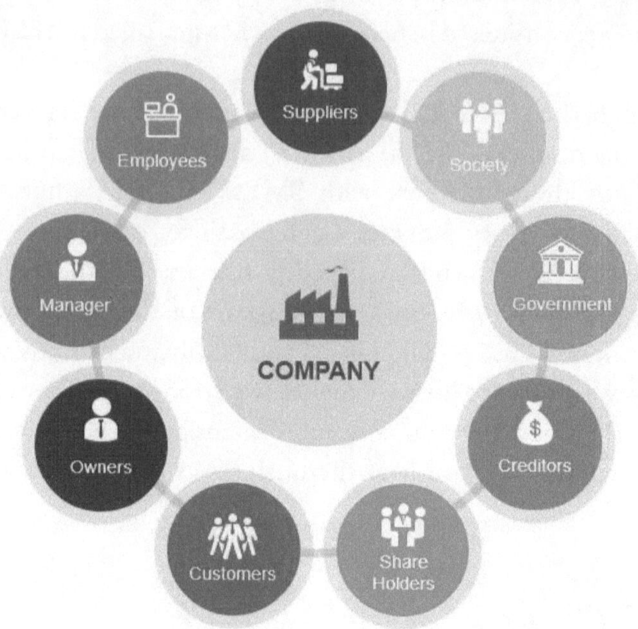

Figure 3 - Typical Business Stakeholders

While SMEs in Africa may not yet be fully attuned to the emphasis being laid on corporate social responsibility (CSR) or environmental and social (E&S) responsibility, this theoretical perspective creates an awareness that stakeholders impact the business and are impacted by the business. In addition, these stakeholders have varying interests and expectations; therefore, in considering corporate governance, the SME should understand how best to interact with its stakeholders to achieve optimum benefit from the interaction. For small businesses, understanding the needs and expectations of the business stakeholders is vital, and could be the first step to extracting value from the value chain.

Resource Dependence Theory

A relatively less examined corporate governance theory is the resource dependence theory.[39] The board is expected to be a provider of resources to the company to enable company performance.[40] The board should provide four basic types of resources in fulfillment of their roles and responsibilities to the company[41]:

(1) strategic advice, counsel, guidance, and know-how (knowledge, skills, and experience),
(2) legitimacy and reputation through their conduct and practices (engendering trust and credibility),
(3) channels for communication between the company and its stakeholders (stakeholder engagement), and
(4) links to other organizations or support by external service providers.

These resources are collectively referred to as *board capital*—in other words, the input that the board invests in the performance of the company.

Resource dependence theory, therefore, advocates for an appropriate board composition that will assure the company of a wide range of resources through their respective social and professional networks.[42] Resource dependence theory is a more successful lens for viewing boards and understanding their (expected) contribution to the company. An owner-managed business that is seeking to diversify needs to focus on bringing on board specific types of directors, based on the resources of board capital that they have.[43] Notably, an attempt at wholesome adoption of the resource dependence theory may be difficult to contemplate for SMEs in Africa. They are just coming to terms with the concept of establishing a functioning board and grappling with the shortage of options for board appointments.

Table 1: Summary of the Theoretical Frameworks

	Agency theory	Stewardship theory	Stakeholder theory	Resource dependence theory
Foundational work	Manne (1965) Jensen and Meckling (1976)	Donaldson (1990a), (1990b); Barney (1990) Davis et al., (1997)	Freeman (1984) Blair (1995)	Pfeffer and Salancik's (1978)
Relationship	Based on the principal-manager relationship: describes the individual-level agent behaviors and the firm-level agency governance mechanisms that are implemented in response.	Based on the principal-manager relationship: describes the individual-level steward behaviors and the firm-level stewardship governance mechanisms that are implemented in response.	Based on the principal-manager relationship: stakeholders are considered to be the real principals of the managers. Relationship with the stakeholders is critical.	The company is an open system, dependent on contingencies in the external environment that the directors embody. Relationship between the company and the board would depend on the resources that each board member brings.
Assumption	Economic model of man	Humanistic model of man	Social/ morality/ ethics	Power and control over resources
Behavior	Opportunistic: individual/ self-serving	Pro-organizational: collective/ other-serving	Social awareness	Strategic resource provision

	Agency theory	**Stewardship theory**	**Stakeholder theory**	**Resource dependence theory**
Governance	Monitoring and incentive systems: mechanisms to curb opportunistic behavior by aligning the interests of the manager with those of the principal	Trust systems: mechanisms to encourage cooperation and involvement to facilitate the natural alignment of interests between the manager and principal	Legitimacy seeking: mechanism to address the interest, expectations, and values of the stakeholders in order to gain the "license to operate"	Focus on board size and composition as indicators of the board's ability to provide critical resources to the firm; boards of directors enable firms to minimize dependence or gain resources
Outcome	Performance by way of cost minimization. Strengthening management incentive systems.	Performance by way of wealth maximization by association with stakeholder.	Performance by way inclusivity.	Performance by way of board resource provision.

	Agency theory	**Stewardship theory**	**Stakeholder theory**	**Resource dependence theory**
Relevance to small business governance	Establishment of control is necessary for business survival; even in situations where the owner manages the business, it is important to establish a relatively simple control and monitoring mechanism. SMEs may lack critical resources for monitoring and adequate separation of roles. An effort to protect the interest of the shareholder through alignment of the interests of agents and shareholders should be the focus of a valid CG framework. The board (or the management team) is usually a key structural tool to curtail managerial excesses capable of jeopardizing the shareholders' interest.	It is expected that in SMEs, there is a unity of direction and of strong command and control (owner-managed). Thus, no real need for excessive role delineation. The CG framework should focus on creating facilitative and empowering structures to enhance operational effectiveness and produce a superior return to shareholders.	Understanding the interests, expectations, and values of an SME, business stakeholders could contribute to business sustainability, as it provides the "license to operate." A valid CG framework should accommodate or address the needs and expectations of key stakeholders.	Small businesses tend to experience a lack of critical resources; therefore, resource provision should be important. Careful selection of directors and managers that can provide needed resources would be valuable. Board (or management team) size, composition, and practices should be considered in the CG framework for SMEs.

Summary of Theoretical Frameworks, adapted from Madison et al. 2016; Letza et al., 2004.

Chapter Summary: Points to Pause and Ponder

- Based on the foregoing, each of the theoretical perspective of corporate governance has a unique contribution to the subject matter and presents some relevance to SME governance.
- It is not essential to rely conclusively on one theoretical framework and disregard others. There is merit in all theoretical perspective, even if they may not apply completely or in the same degree in all situations for SMEs.
- A combination of elements of different theoretical perspectives gives a robust understanding of the underlying dynamics and under which conditions each perspective is more applicable.
- Expectedly, there is no single (one-size-fits-all) governance model that provides sufficiently for all types and forms of SMEs, as SMEs are usually at different stages in their business life cycle, and therefore, adaptation is essential.
- Corporate governance systems are often (and should be) shaped by various factors, including business cultures, sector, size, timelines, and business life cycles.

CHAPTER 3

ELEMENTS OF GOOD CORPORATE GOVERNANCE

In furthering the discussion of corporate governance, it is important to base the discussion on an existing model of corporate governance that outlines its key elements. To develop a framework relevant to small and growing businesses, a combination of years of professional experience, a search of the literature, and empirical research has been leveraged.

The elements (building blocks) of corporate governance draw from the corporate governance framework of the International Finance Corporation (IFC), the largest global development institution focusing exclusively on the private sector in developing countries. The framework is based on the revised OECD Corporate Governance Principles. This framework has been adopted and is being used extensively across the globe, covering middle- and low-income countries.

There are six key elements that companies need to pay attention to in order to maintain an effective corporate governance framework.

1. Commitment to good CG principles
2. The decision-making body
3. Control systems and processes
4. Transparency and disclosure
5. Owners/shareholders and family
6. Stakeholders engagement

These six elements of good corporate governance are described below.

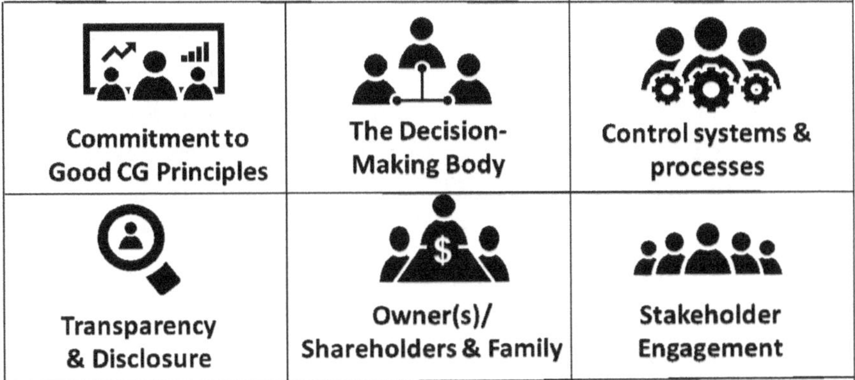

Figure 4 - Elements of Effective Corporate Governance Framework

Commitment to Good CG Principles

Good corporate governance requires the demonstration of a clear focus on establishing effective structures and processes for achieving the benefits of good CG. Structures, policies, and procedures are required as the backbone of any viable company. However, commitment to good corporate governance is more than merely putting structures, policies, and procedures in place. It is the behavior and culture that permeates the company and the level of acceptance of the business benefits of good corporate governance practices. There is a correlation between the *commitment to* and *entrenchment of* corporate governance practices in a company.[44]

A company's willingness to go above and beyond regulatory requirements and to look beyond compliance gives an indication of its level of commitment. Furthermore, a strong commitment can be noticed by the company's shareholders, potential investors, and stakeholders. Practical personal experience shows that the ability to understand the company, to solicit good will, to access lower cost of capital, and to enhance the company's reputation are all improved and reinforced by demonstrable commitment to good corporate governance principles.

Commitment to good corporate governance lends itself to addressing the tone at the top that drives the organizational culture and is significantly impacted by the owner/CEO/board of directors. "Culture" has been defined as "a set of values, symbols and rituals shared by the members of a specific organization, which describe the way things are done." Commitment to corporate governance is the conceptual foundation of organizational culture, which, in a small businesses, is influenced by the owner/manager.[45]

For very small (or stage-one) businesses, it is important to identify core functions with the aim of setting up policies around them. These core functions form the basis of the organizational chart with clear reporting lines. A business plan is also necessary to provide context. As the business matures, the core processes should be documented. Formal documentation provides direction to the owner/manager, guides the actions of the employees, and demonstrates to other stakeholders that the business is maturing.

The Decision-Making Body (Board of Directors and Management Team)

The existence of a competent, legitimate, well-structured, and effective board, including considerations related to the composition, structure, and procedures of the company, are part of a good corporate governance framework. According to the agency theory, the board acts in the best interests of the company and its shareholders.[46] An effective, professional and independent board of directors is believed to influence corporate performance and is an essential pillar of good corporate governance. In the *King IV Report*, this is described as the "governing body." The governing body has the responsibility (and is accountable for) leading the organization in an ethical manner to achieve positive outcomes.

While there is more focus on large companies to have well-constituted boards, even in a small business, having an independent board should not be disregarded, particularly as the board provides strategic direction to the company. The board is the focal or critical pillar of corporate governance because it has the responsibility to monitor the activities of the company, set the company's strategy, and appoint and oversee senior management and the company's financial operations.[47]

Small private companies in emerging markets have been found to report higher return on investment because of the presence of outside directors.[48] While the board cannot substitute for talented professional managers or change the economic environment in which a company operates, it can influence the performance of the company through its strategic oversight and control over management.[49] It would appear from studies in both academic research and corporate practice that there is a relationship between the existence and performance of the board of directors and the business's performance.[50]

Invariably, for both large and small companies, the ability of the board to deliver on its role aids in the survival of the company. When making financial investment decisions, investors and financiers consider the existence of a board. This is not to disregard the management team; having the right top management teams adds value to decision-making as it also determines the strategic performance of the company.[51]

Figure 5 - Alternative Routes to a Board

Small businesses can employ several options to develop a board of directors. The most straightforward one is building the board of directors from scratch, by inviting representatives of key shareholders, select executives, and external advisors. Or, if the board exists on paper but is not functional, the company may "activate" the paper board (i.e., make it properly functional). However, for many businesses, this is a big step, as it involves trusting outsiders with key business information and strategic decision-making. There are two other options that allow the owner to test the waters gradually and practice good board procedures.

1. The company can test the waters with an advisory board, perfecting the procedures, practices, and adjusting the skills mix. The advisory board then serves as the basis for establishing the proper board of directors. Most, or all the advisory board members may be invited to join the board. Key members of the executive committee are also invited to join. Such a board is typically dominated by outside directors and has a high degree of independence from management.

2. The board can evolve from the executive committee. In this case, the companies may have special strategic executive sessions (once every two to three months), where external advisors may be invited (or other shareholders, if applicable) to discuss long-term issues and opportunities. Participants in such strategic sessions later become members of the board of directors. Such boards have strong knowledge of operations but tend to be dominated by management, so extra effort is needed to ensure proper oversight functions. Adding nonexecutive/ independent directors is crucial.

The issue of independence on the board of an SME often creates tension with SMEs. Although it is advisable to have a board consisting of a majority of nonexecutives, of which the majority is independent, it is not always possible with SMEs—especially when SMEs are family-run enterprises. To address the tension, the South Africa's *King IV Report* suggests that the board of such a company consider appointing a nonexecutive director with the necessary skills and competence to ensure the mix of executive and nonexecutive directors is appropriate. However, a small business is sometimes unable to bear the cost of such an appointment. Therefore, if the appointment of such an individual is not financially viable, the King IV Report suggests that an individual who meets these criteria be regularly consulted until the appointment of such an individual is feasible. This will also ensure objective decision-making, removing the occurrence of emotion-based decision-making.

Control System and Processes

Internal control is a process that is developed by management, with the main objective being to reasonably ensure the ability of the enterprise to safeguard its assets, the integrity of information, and compliance.[52] An effective risk-management process is one that is designed to identify, evaluate, and manage business-related risks in a structured and systematic manner.[53] These business risks could arise from internal or external risk factors. These definitions provide a robust perspective of the control environment, which appears to be a very important requirement for businesses (both large and small).

External board members help encourage more independent practices in the internal control systems, which should result in more accountability and higher profitability through better risk management.[54] A functional internal control system is a critical component of an organization's governance system and is considered the foundation for sound operations.[55] The internal audit function in an organization contributes significantly to improve corporate governance practices,[56] specifically, it plays a role in the prevention of fraud.[57]

The focus should be on developing more structured, consistent, and formal management control processes across the company to support its objectives. A lack of or weak control system and processes contributes significantly to poor financial performance. A strong internal control system is able to support sustained business development; conversely, a small business with weak internal controls is vulnerable to risks that may be detrimental to its survival and sustainability.[58]

At a rudimentary level, the control system and processes should include basic bookkeeping and cash-flow management, ensuring that cash sources and bank accounts are separate from those of the founders. As the business matures, relevant accounting policies should be documented and followed, and a basic system to record and track sales and accounts should be set up. At a more advanced stage, business units should be established, and basic internal-audit activities should be performed and reported. At this stage, an effective and professional finance officer should be in place, and an effort should be made to get the financial statements audited by external auditors.

Transparency and Disclosure

The concept of transparency and disclosure relates to the ready availability of timely, accurate, relevant, complete, and actionable information equally to all shareholders and, as appropriate, to other stakeholders, including regulators. Transparency and disclosure practices tend to create a structured discourse between companies and their shareholders and stakeholders. The discourse enables the external parties to better understand, through disclosed information, the company's strategic and operational goals, including key performance indicators and critical success factors for achieving the goals.[59]

Availability and disclosure of information on a business's product and services, as well as finance and governance structure, are often requirements for attracting finance for business growth.[60] Institutional investors are paying more attention to corporate transparency and governance disclosure practices, even for SMEs, and better information disclosure is likely to boost investor interest.[61] Put differently, appropriate disclosure by SMEs increases the investors' confidence in the company, thereby improving their chances of obtaining funding from investors or financial institutions.[62] In fact, inadequate disclosure is proof of poor business management and lack of financial discipline by investment teams.[63] Disclosure practices are sometimes influenced by cultural factors,[64] and the culture of the organization that drives disclosure is often determined by the board. Financial markets are faced with the problem of information asymmetry (i.e., the difficulty of evaluating the quality of a company's management framework and protection against moral hazards). Hence, transparency and disclosure are essential.

Most SMEs in emerging markets find it difficult to maintain adequate financial record keeping, which often results in the failure to make good use of the available financial information or demonstrate the viability of their business to potential financiers.[65] Undeniably, good record keeping does not have to be expensive considering the availability of various reasonably priced electronic media for information management (storage, processing, and retrieval).

For very small or stage-one businesses, the initial focus should be on formalizing the business. Therefore, basic financial data should be generated, based on which financial records will be prepared for all purposes. To professionalize the business, monthly bank account reconciliation should be prepared and given to all founders. It is also important to develop a profile of the business for marketing purposes. Financial statements, in keeping with national accounting standards, audited by an external auditor, are a staple of basic SME governance. Also, key nonfinancial information may be disclosed to the public. This is a precursor to generating quarterly financial statements and comprehensive performance reports, at a more advanced stage. Financial reporting will have to be done according to the International Financial Reporting Standards (IFRS), and annual report should be available at this stage.

Owners/Shareholders and Family

Proper treatment of all shareholders, including protection from abuse by larger investors and company insiders, is critical. Due to the agency's theoretical perspective, and in an environment with widely dispersed ownership, emphasis is often placed on the protection of shareholder rights, particular the rights of minority investors.[66] Protection of shareholders (external investors) is important in many countries because there is a risk that the controlling shareholders or managers could expropriate the minority shareholders and creditors, thus putting at risk their investment in the company.[67]

There are various ways that the rights of minority shareholders can be abused, including fraudulent practices that can jeopardize returns, transfer pricing, tunneling, and related party transactions.[68] It is therefore important, if a company wants to attract finance, to establish mechanisms that would protect the interests of external parties. In different countries, investors protection rules come from different sources, including company law and accounting standards.[69] The aim should be finding a point of alignment for the incentives of various shareholders (controlling and minority, insiders and outsiders).[70]

Treatment of shareholders/protection of minority shareholders' rights is often a challenge in emerging market scenario where the legal system is weak, and laws are not readily enforceable. In most African countries, shareholding is highly concentrated and usually held by founders or members of the same family; however, tight family control is not a good safeguard for minority shareholders.

Family business governance provides a system of process and structures put in place at the highest level of the business, family, and ownership to make the best possible decisions regarding the direction of the business and assurance of accountability and control. In a well-developed family business, this involves understanding how the business and its governance structure interact with the family and its structures.

In some instances, agency problems can be exacerbated by family-ownership dynamics. Therefore, a set of mechanisms needs to be established through which outside investors can be protected against expropriation by the controlling shareholders or managers. At a minimum, the roles and responsibilities of the founders and a basic understanding of the roles of other family members should be clear. There should be a forum (such as a shareholders' meeting) to discuss major decisions and future plans. And in between meetings, all shareholders need to be kept informed of company matters. Dispute-resolution mechanisms for shareholder-related disputes should be articulated. In *chapter 11 - consideration for governance of family businesses,* I provided some insights on family businesses governance.

Stakeholders Engagement

Stakeholders of a business have been described as "those groups without whose support the organization would cease to exist."[71] Good corporate governance leads to development of a framework that provides adequate protection to the interests of stakeholders and reinforces the fiduciary responsibilities of those vested with the authority to act on behalf of the stakeholders. A business manager should ensure that stakeholders with valid and viable interest in a company's business are fully taken into account in decision-making and in disclosure of information.

In the stakeholders' approach, the role of the board or decision-making body is even more important, as it will not only control that the managers' main decisions comply with the shareholders' interests, but also that all the other stakeholders are satisfied in order to keep the company going on. To ensure *corporate legitimacy* there should be a mechanism to address the interests and expectations of the stakeholders in order to gain the *"license to operate.*" From some point of view, the stakeholders' approach is a way to change the focus of the managers from an excessive attention to the short-term financial results and to redirect their attention to the long-term overall performance of the business.

There needs to be a structured way of engaging with the company's stakeholders. It is essential as a start, for the company to demonstrated awareness of its stakeholders as potentially interested parties in its business. At a more advanced stage, specific reports may need to be provided to key stakeholders, there will be formal mechanism to address stakeholder matters and maintain a communication channel.

Chapter Summary: Points to Pause and Ponder

- There are six key elements of an effective corporate governance system. These include commitment to good corporate governance, the board of directors and management team, the control systems and processes, transparency and disclosure practices, the owner/shareholders and family dimension, and engagement of stakeholders.
- These elements enable small businesses to maintain better and stronger system of internal control and accountability, transparency, and strategic vision through participation of outside experts on the board, allowing the owner to focus more on strategic directions and the expansion of the business rather than day-to-day operations and ability to attract better managers.
- Engagement with stakeholder provides a company with the *license to operate.*
- Establishing these elements as early as possible places the small business in good stead to attract employees, investors, and customers.
- Corporate governance provides the frameworks to help companies of all sizes achieve long-term business success.
- Corporate governance is not a synonym for a large corporate board, but it is about good business practices at all levels.
- Companies need to be accountable and transparent even when they are small and privately owned.
- For SMEs, it should be noted that corporate governance is mainly about improving business efficiency and performance

SECTION TWO

DYNAMICS OF SME BUSINESSES

CHAPTER 4

SMALL- AND MEDIUM-SIZED BUSINESSES

There is currently no universal agreement on the definition and description of small businesses, popularly referred to as small- and medium-sized enterprises (SME). Definitions of what constitutes a small business vary quite widely from country to country and even within single countries, depending on the business sector concerned. Different definitions, descriptions, and classifications have been given to this category of business by different authors. The determinant or criteria of an SME often depends on the character of the relevant host country and the profile of its own particular corporate sector, from which a relative measure of an SME is then typically made, sometimes on a rather arbitrary basis.

Generally, one of the main criteria for determining whether a business is an SME is the number of employees. In addition, some countries consider either the value of the company's assets or the size of revenues, typically denominated in the local currency. In cases where a currency value is cited (either for assets or revenues), any marked inflation can become a problem for the SME definition over time. In some countries, the criteria for SMEs are updated occasionally. The form of ownership profile, type of legal entity, or origin of the company are also sometimes included in creating the definition.

Some countries distinguish between a microenterprise and a small enterprise, while others—by not setting a floor for SME size—effectively include microenterprises within their SME umbrella definition. The above notwithstanding, most SME definitions pertain to businesses that are formal in nature and have been registered in some manner, and they exclude small-scale, informal family enterprises.

From another viewpoint, small businesses can be broadly categorized based on two features, "economic" and "statistical." Under the economic characterization, a firm is regarded as small if it meets the following three criteria:

1. It has a relatively small share of the market.
2. It is managed by owners, or part-owners, in a personalized way and not through the medium of a formalized management structure.
3. It is independent and not part of a larger enterprise.

The statistical characterization, on the other hand, is used in three main areas:

1. Quantifying the size of the small business sector and its contribution to the Gross Domestic Product (GDP), employment and exports.
2. Comparing the extent to which the small firm sector's economic contribution has changed over time.
3. In a cross-country comparison of the small firms' economic contribution.

These definitions, however, have a few weaknesses. For example, the economic definition, which states that a small business is managed by its owners or part-owners in a *personalized way* and not through the medium of a formal management structure, is incompatible with its statistical definition of a small manufacturing firm, which might have up to two hundred employees. In any case, the definition of small businesses by size is necessary, but it is not sufficient for an understanding of a sector where the realities are not only complex but also very dynamic. In this book, the term "small businesses" will be used as an umbrella description for small, and medium enterprises, lest we be overly concerned with the technicalities of each type.

The International Perspective

The British Department of Trade and Industry indicates that the best description of a small firm remains that used by the Bolton Committee in its 1971 *Report on Small Firms*. This stated that a small firm is an independent business, managed by its owner or part owners and having a small market share.[72]

In 2003, the European Union Commission issued an official journal concerning the definition of micro, small, and medium-sized enterprises. The recommendation was that "the category of micro, small and medium-sized enterprises (MSMEs) is made up of enterprises which employ fewer than 250 persons and which have an annual turnover not exceeding EUR 50 million, and/or an annual balance sheet total not exceeding EUR 43 million."[73]

In the United States, the Small Business Administration sets small business criteria based on industry, ownership structure, revenue, and number of employees (which, in some circumstances, may be as high as 1,500, although the cap is typically 500). The threshold of fewer than ten employees is used for small offices.

The Inter-American Development Bank defines SMEs as having a maximum of one hundred employees and less than $3 million in revenue. In Europe, they are defined as having manpower fewer than 250 employees, and the United States defines them as consisting of fewer than 500 employees. The World Bank defines SMEs as those enterprises with a maximum of 300 employees, $15 million in annual revenue, and $15 million in assets.

In the Asia-Pacific region, there is a wide diversity of SME definitions; this is because SMEs are not uniform across the region in either size or shape.[74] In many countries in this region, the definition firstly depends on the business sector. Other factors typically considered include, the number of employees, annual sales turnover, and fixed capital size.[75]

The business categorization from the international perspective would appear to present a relatively larger business than those seen in Africa. In addition, corporate governance mechanisms are more developed and institutionalized, and the legal framework supports the enforcement of corporate governance practices.

The African Perspective

In Africa, the definitions, descriptions and classifications of small businesses would be pitched far lower compared to the international perspective.

The National Small Business Act of South Africa of 1996, as amended in 2003, describes an SME as "a separate and distinct entity managed by one owner or more, including its branches or subsidiaries if any is predominantly carried out in any sector or sub-sector of the economy mentioned in the schedule of size standards and can be classified as a SME by satisfying the criteria mentioned in the schedule of size standards." The schedule of size standards stipulates that small businesses have one to forty-nine employees, maximum turnover of R51m, and a balance sheet size of R19m. Medium-size businesses are those with 51–200 employees, a maximum turnover of R13m, and a balance sheet size of R5m.

A study by the Small and Medium Enterprises Development Agency of Nigeria (SMEDAN) (2010) revealed that most SMEs in Nigeria employ ten to forty-nine employees. The Central Bank of Nigeria, in one of its communiques of the special monetary policy, acknowledged the existence of several definitions of SMEs. One of such definitions states that an enterprise that has an asset base (excluding land) of between N5 million to N500 million and a labor force of between 11 and 300 belongs to the SME subsector. According to the SME Equity Investment Scheme, an SME is defined as any enterprise with a maximum asset base of N1.5 billion (excluding land and working capital), with no lower or upper limit of staff.[76]

In Ghana, the National Board for Small Scale Industries (NBSSI) defines SMEs as enterprises that employ twenty-nine or fewer workers. Under the Micro and Small Enterprise Act of 2012, microenterprises have a maximum annual turnover of KES 500,000 and employ fewer than ten people. Small enterprises have between KES 500,000 and 5 million annual turnover and employ ten to forty-nine people. However, medium enterprises are not covered under the act but have been reported as comprising of enterprises with a turnover of between KES 5 million and 800 million and employing fifty to ninety-nine employees.

The official national definitions of SMEs by maximum number of employees for Morocco is 200, while for Egypt, Malawi, Tanzania and a few other African countries it is fifty.

A Less Quantitative Perspective

There are divergent views about the quantitative measures (employees, assets, and turnover) by which SMEs should be defined and the benchmark for such definitions. To a large extent, SMEs are more meaningfully defined by their functional and behavioral attributes than by quantifications. These functional characteristics are important to monitor but presents a degree of impracticality in quantifying such attributes for large numbers of companies across different economic climates. I read an article[77], in which the authors after more than two decades of investing in SMEs on four continents, described certain unique qualitative attributes of SMEs, which could be considered proxies for a quantitative definition. SMEs are in general:

- formal, meaning that they are registered with government ministries or other registration bodies;
- obligated to pay taxes and social security charges, as they are generally too large or visible in the community to avoid paying such governmental charges;
- able to allow their employees to take sick leave and vacations while receiving compensation;
- able and generally willing to provide formal skills training for their employees and providing such training for a substantial percentage of such employees;
- able to finance accounts receivables;
- able to invest in capital with a payback of longer than 12 months; and,
- more often managed by their owners, more centralized in their management, with substantially weaker delegation and departmentalization;
- more focused on short-term needs and medium-term survival than on long-term profitability or market share;
- less able, and less inclined, to prepare and follow business plans;

- less technologically sophisticated and slower to take advantage of available and affordable technology;
- more flexible and able to adapt quickly to changes in the economic and regulatory environment;
- more often only able to hire (and therefore compelled to train) unskilled workers who generally will not meet the hiring criteria of large firms; and
- more dependent upon personal relationships between management and workers and between management and customers.

The attributes listed above may not apply to every enterprise, but they provide a more inclusive description of SMEs than employees, turnover and assets, which tend to exclude businesses which are either too large or too small to be characterized this way.

Small Businesses Matter

It is worth reiterating that small businesses are vital to economies around the world. Formal SMEs in high-income countries contribute almost 50 percent of GDP on average.[78] According to the Organization for Economic Co-operation and Development (OECD), small businesses create employment and income, they respond to new or niched demands, and they enhance our social inclusion.[79] According to Supachai Panitchpakdi, when he was the secretary-general of the United Nations Conference on Trade and Development (UNCTAD) in 2006, "SMEs are a source of employment, competition, economic dynamism, and innovation; they stimulate the entrepreneurial spirit and the diffusion of skills. Because they enjoy a wider geographical presence than big companies, SMEs also contribute to better income distribution."

Countries in Africa have often been described as having low national incomes, poor economic policies, high commodity dependence, and weak institutions and governance; accordingly, these attributes make them more likely to perform poorly economically. In 2019, UNCTAD[80] reported that about 89 percent of African countries depend precariously on commodities. Commodity-dependent countries have long been victims of booms and busts, leaving little behind. To provide sustainable opportunities for its citizens, an economy needs a diversified base that will serve consumers while fostering local comparative advantages, creating jobs and sustaining the global economy. SMEs play a central role in poverty reduction as "connectors" of local economic activity.

SMEs are fast becoming the dominant form of business ventures in the African continent. With high unemployment rates, people are turning toward informal and formal small businesses to sustain their livelihood. It is therefore not surprising that small businesses play a critical role in the economies of countries in Africa. SMEs tend to dominate the corporate community in all countries, at least in terms of company registrations, if not always in terms of aggregate size, and have been known to represent a vital part in the economy of every country.[81] There has been a significant increase in the activities of SMEs in Africa in the last thirty years, and this has been attributed to the fact that interest-bearing investment opportunities are few and far between.[82]

To buttress the importance of SMEs to the national economy, it has been reported that in Nigeria, there are a total of 41.5 million micro, small, and medium enterprises making up the growth sector,[83] contributing about 47.8 percent to the Nigerian GDP.[84] In South Africa, SMEs account for about 91 percent of the formal business entities, contributing to about 57 percent of GDP and providing almost 60 percent of employment.[85] Specifically, in South Africa, SMEs contribute 56 percent of private sector employment and 36 percent of the gross domestic product.[86]

In Ghana, small businesses form a greater percentage of business enterprises. SMEs in Ghana have been noted to provide about 85 percent of manufacturing employment and are also believed to contribute about 70 percent to Ghana's GDP and account for about 92 percent of businesses. SMEs account for about 75% of employment and 80% of GDP in Egypt.

In 2014, 80 percent of jobs created in Kenya were dominated by these enterprises.[87] According to a report by the United Nations Industrial Development Organization (UNIDO), SMEs represent over 90 percent of private business and contribute to more than 50 percent of employment and of GDP in most African countries.[88] Around the world, it is generally accepted that small businesses are the main engine of job creation [89]

There appears to be substantial evidence that even in countries with large corporations, such as the United States, SMEs contribute a very substantial percentage to employment opportunities, supplying goods and services to consumers and large businesses.[90] Specifically for the economic contribution dimension, in the United States, small businesses have generated 66 percent of all new jobs for the past four decades.[91] The rapid transformation of high-performing Asian countries, such as India, Malaysia, Indonesia, Taiwan, and Hong Kong, also provide evidence that small businesses are major catalysts in economic development.

It is therefore vital to consider development in the SME sector. In Nigeria, economic policies and programs have recognized SMEs as the most popular types of business, particularly based on outcomes related to income generation, poverty reduction, and employment.[92] A research report on SME firms' performance in Nigeria also alluded to the fact that SME performance forms a very important part of the Nigerian economy.[93]Similarly, in Ghana, governments at all levels have undertaken different initiatives to encourage and support the growth of SMEs.[94]

The fact that there is interest in ensuring the development of SMEs is good, but corporate governance must be taken into cognizance by all and sundry. Corporate governance provides a framework in promoting the triple objective of transparency, fairness, and accountability, leading to profit maximization, promoting investors' confidence, and ultimately creating jobs. The importance of corporate governance to the development of SMEs makes this book a good resource for small businesses, investors, and policymakers.

Performance of Small Businesses

Strong organizational performance, profitability and growth are typical business goals of owners and managers of small businesses. In addition, policymakers and governments are eager to support the performance of these small businesses, because, as described above, small businesses play a vital role in the growth and development of the economies.[95]

The performance and growth of SMEs are major drivers and indicators of the "level of industrialization, modernization, urbanization, gainful and meaningful employment for all those who are able and willing to work, equitable distribution of income, the welfare, income per capital and quality of life enjoyed by the citizenry."[96]

Entrepreneurship and the ability to start up small businesses are not factors in short supply in Africa, but successful entrepreneurs and enterprises form only a fraction of the present population of small businesses. The ability of small businesses to provide the ascribed economic benefits is significantly determined by the health of the business and the business environment in which they are obliged to operate.

When conditions are less than conducive for development and growth, small businesses remain stunted or much less dynamic in their operations. This explains in large part why attention is often placed on various global indicators that attempt to measure and compare the business environments in different countries. Good indicators have a genuine benefit in providing a basis for effective comparison across countries, which will help policymakers to intervene.

Despite the noted contributions of small businesses to national economies, their failure rate is high across the globe. Understandably, some SMEs will go on to great things in later life, while most will probably achieve more modest goals, and sadly, some will come to a premature death for one reason or another. In general, at least half of all new companies close within two years of commencing operations. One study in the United States found that 40 percent of manufacturing firms fail within five years of beginning operations.

Similarly, in South Africa, 50–80 percent of businesses fail within the first five years.[97] According to the Kenya National Bureau of Statistics (NBS),[98] three out of five businesses fail within the first few months of operation. Generally, there is inadequate data to determine a firm failure rate for SMEs in Africa. Few companies go through the regulatory process of formal business closure. Instead, many go into a state of suspended animation, which has the attraction of being able to revive the company at a later stage should conditions change for the better. In addition, while countries are often quite zealous at recording and reporting the birth of new companies (startups), they tend to be much less focused on recording company failures and closures. Clearly, survival a key concern for SMEs.

Another challenge that SMEs have is the difficulty in attracting funds for expansion. As a result, they tend to rely heavily on personal sources and short-term financing, which is very costly. Several of the factors that cause SMEs to fail can be traced to failure to adopt good corporate governance.

When the set of rules and processes that form the corporate governance mechanism of a business are ineffective or fail, the consequences for the business can be disastrous. Therefore, greater attention should be paid to assisting SMEs to understand and adopt good governance practices to safeguard their business.

True development of the SME sector cannot be realistically sustained without strengthening the businesses. Adoption of good corporate governance practices, even proportionally, and placing the focus on basic principles such as ethical leadership, independence, performance management, and succession planning can provide several benefits to an SME. It will, by extension, enhance the contribution of the SMEs to the economies in Africa.

Developing the SME sector is important because one of the best ways to address unemployment, which plagues Africa today, is to leverage the employment creation potential of small businesses and to promote small business development.[99] Countries in Africa stand to benefit significantly through integration and skills development of its large yet unproductive informal sector—SMEs.

Chapter Summary: Points to Pause and Ponder

- SMEs represent more than 80 percent of total business establishments in Africa. In the private sector, 70 percent of the working population are being employed by SMEs.
- The factor for determining whether a business is an SME should not be solely the quantitative but should include more qualitative factors.
- SMEs are a source of employment, competition, economic dynamism, and innovation; they stimulate the entrepreneurial spirit and the diffusion of skills.
- Despite the noted contributions of small businesses to national economies, the failure rate of SMEs in Africa is high.
- Survival is a key concern for SMEs
- SMEs have difficulty attracting funds for expansion. As a result, they tend to rely heavily on personal sources and short-term financing, which is very costly.

CHAPTER 5
STAGES OF GROWTH AND GOVERNANCE EVOLUTION

SMEs vary widely in size and capacity for growth.[100] Small businesses evolve and will go through different stages of growth. Sometimes, these stages are well-defined. At other times, they merge seamlessly. They are characterized by independence of action, differing organizational structures, and varied management styles. It is also important to note that the stages are dynamic—a company might be "between stages," in the process of moving from one stage to another. In reviewing the various literature relevant to the small business growth, coupled with my own personal research study and work experience, I have identified several important viewpoints on the topic of small business growth and evolution.

No two businesses are exactly alike, and that means the journey of every business will be different. But no matter the type of business or industry, there are points of similarity, which means that most businesses experience common problems arising at similar stages in their development.

There are five common stages of growth that every business will experience, each with its own set of challenges. A description of these stages should increase understanding of the nature, characteristics, and problems of small businesses. Each SME is unique, ranging from a corner dairy shop with two or three minimum-wage workers to a multimillion-dollar software company experiencing a relatively good annual rate of growth.

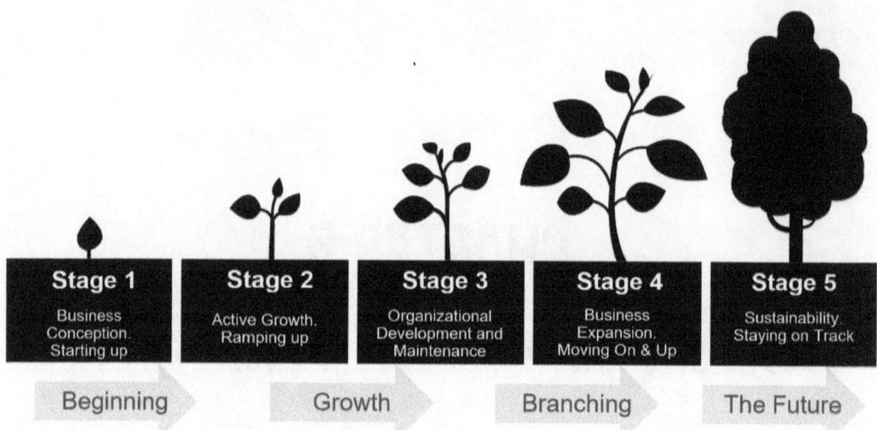

Figure 6 - Stages of Small Business Growth

This chapter provides a description of the five stages, and owners and managers of small businesses will do well to become conversant as well as prepared. The more knowledgeable and prepared one is in advance for each stage of growth, understanding the challenges that might come along with it, the greater the chances are for a successful business in the long run. Such an understanding can help owners assess current challenges, such as the need to hire and train second-level managers to maintain planned growth. It can also help owners and managers of small businesses anticipate the key requirements of various stages, such as the excessive time commitment for owners during the startup period and the need for delegation and changes in their managerial roles when companies become larger and more complex.

There is no academic agreement on the number, the sequence, the timeline, and the movement of stages, but there is broad consensus that the conditions vary along similar patterns as the small business matures. Interestingly, no single factor defines the exact point of stage transition, but rather the combination of stage characteristics will indicate the status of the SME's primary growth stage.

Evolution of Corporate Governance Mechanisms

Corporate governance should be an integral business culture and way of working rather than simply an adherence to a set of rules. It must stem from the company itself and be proportionate with its development. For each stage of a company's life cycle, a governance system must exist to help the company meet its objectives. It also dictates the relationship between the business owners and all other stakeholders, in order to achieve company objectives and preserve the rights of all stakeholders.[101]

Corporate governance will and should evolve as a company grows and expands. A strong and well-functioning governance arrangement adds value at every stage of a company's growth and development. The key factors that should determine the appropriate corporate governance framework for SMEs should be the following:

- ownership structure/company type
- size (employees, revenue)
- stage of growth of the business
- nature and complexity of the business
- strategy of the business (where the business is going)

A good corporate governance structure will allow the SME owner/manager to ensure that growth of the business occurs smoothly, with minimal confusion about responsibilities. The following are a few things to consider when setting up the governance structure:

- the need to create and delegate authority
- the importance of developing clear policies and procedures
- the value of having adequate control mechanisms
- the responsibility to manage employees and ensure accountability

The business environment is complex and tends to change rapidly. It is characterized by the emergence of new risks and opportunities. The corporate governance system should be developed to align with the business needs, addressing the risks and taking advantage of the opportunities. The nature of corporate governance practices required for guidance and control varies for each stage of a business life cycle, and these will be described in tandem with each stage of growth.

The corporate governance practices suggested at the early stages emphasize the role of management practice more than the board practice, which is traditionally understood as corporate governance. This is because issues pertaining to leadership by management would need to be addressed before leadership by a board can be effectively implemented. However, corporate governance encapsulates practically every sphere of management, from strategy to action plans and internal controls to performance measurement and corporate disclosure.

In describing the stages of business growth, some corporate governance practices will be suggested. These are not meant to be exhaustive or encompass all situations and businesses, but they are meant to encourage SMEs to think about corporate governance and provide practical ideas on how to initiate a functional framework.

The typical characteristics and challenges of each stage are described below. (Note that these stages and related corporate governance practices are only illustrative; actual governance evolution and company structure will, of course, depend on each SME).

Stage One: Business Conception. Starting Up

The first stage is the conception or birth of a new business. At this stage, most small businesses are focused on business startup arrangements, developing the product, exploring the markets, and finding customers. The focus of the business is delivering the product or service to customers.

With dedicated focus and limited resources, small businesses typically put little effort into establishing organizational structures systematically. The business operations are straightforward and simple; therefore, an informal and agile approach to managing them works well for the entrepreneur. The prevalent management style is purely individualistic, which means that, to a large extent, the owner and the business are effectively one and the same.

The business is growing organically, with systems designed on the go, and distinct roles are defined as individuals lend a hand as needed to get the job done. The owner wears two hats simultaneously—the visioneer (having the overall vision) and the executor (making things happen). The company's strategy is simply to remain stay in business, as studies have shown that about 80 percent of new businesses fail during this stage.

The owner is the major supplier of energy, direction, and, with relatives and friends, capital. Systems and formal planning are minimal to nonexistent. This is also because the company's product development and agility are top of mind for the owner, and formal rules are deemed to slow things down. There is also the fear that if the business owner rushes into delegation, he or she might lose control.

Potential Governance Challenges

- long-term investment goals but short-term financing capacity
- solo decision-making and overreliance on the founder, creating a key-person risk
- poor cash-flow management
- pricing products or services too high or too low
- mixing of family, personal and business interests, including money
- not preparing a realistic budget
- lack of formal processes and systems

Suggested Corporate Governance Stance at the Conception or Startup Stage

Corporate governance is not always top of mind for business owners and managers at the outset, as they are usually preoccupied with building and scaling the business. Applying governance principles at this stage ensures that governance becomes an integral part of the business and not merely construed as laws and legislations to be ticked off. Most incorporated SMEs have a board of at least two persons. However, the board is realistically a paper board that merely rubber-stamps every proposal or decision of the owner/manager.

This first stage of establishing a business has a significant impact on the shape and culture of governance. The right action at this stage ensures business continuity and a strong governance culture in order to achieve an effective and mature governance system in the future, and it develops along with it.

It is important to consider the following corporate governance practices:

- Consider an advisory board or find a trusted strategic business advisor
- develop a formal business plan and draw up a strategy
- craft a simple organizational structure (this will usually evolve very quickly)
- determine whom to involve in decision-making or engage informal external advisers as required
- maintain basic bookkeeping records
- create a budget and use it
- develop the cash-flow records (capturing inflows and outflows)
- separate business bank accounts from that of the owner's
- establish the necessary regulatory requirements and seek compliance
- draft a shareholders' agreement/partnership agreement

Stage Two: Active Growth. Ramping Up

The business is picking up momentum and can demonstrate that it is a workable business entity. The organization is still relatively simple, and the business owner-cum-manager is starting to build a team. Decision-making is still solely dependent on the owner. The company is rapidly growing in resources and complexity. However, this growth often remains largely organic and unplanned, being based on a broad vision of the owner but with little attention to the development of a defined strategy.

The business may begin expanding, with growing employee numbers but little or no change to the business structures and processes. As employees and/or contractors increase, human capital issues become increasingly apparent. There are situations where, due to a pressing need to meet rising customer demands, the owner hires too many people (sometimes these are family members and close friends), assigning them to roles outside of their experience and qualifications. SMEs find it easier or more convenient to build structures, functions, and processes around available people as opposed to looking for professionals or specially qualified people to handle key roles and perform certain functions. Reporting lines, authorities, and responsibilities remain vaguely defined.

Certain areas of the business now require a degree of formality. These include business strategy, structures and policies, and control systems. There is a need to balance the preference for flexibility with the growing demand of the business for formality. The entrepreneur can be pulled in different directions as he or she struggles to focus on strategic development, seek new opportunities for growth, and run the business operations. Internal controls begin to emerge to deal with increased delegation, growth, and complexity, but the controls remain rudimentary and fragmented. In discussions with SME owners who are in this stage, many of them have shared feelings of helplessness. They testify to being pulled in different directions and crippled by the daily grind to keep the company afloat.

Potential Governance Challenges

- solo or unilateral decision-making
- weak people management, siloed organization
- rudimentary and fragmented internal control systems
- inadequate cash-flow planning
- overwhelmed operations
- misalignment between supply and demand

Suggested Corporate Governance Stance at the Active Growth or Ramp-up Stage

Governance practices at this stage must be built on practices established in the previous stage. It should be supportive for any growth in order to generate greater revenue by broadening the customer base. The required governance practices must consider the direction of the company, to achieve its strategy and maintain a supportive supervisory level.

It is important to consider the following corporate governance practices:

- create an outline of standard policies and processes

- develop a framework of crucial decisions required to manage the business
- decide on authority limits of key personnel
- establish accounting policies and reports needed internally and externally
- establish monthly bank account reconciliation reporting processes
- establish cash control mechanisms
- formalize shareholder agreements/partnership agreement
- prepare financial statements and audit per national accounting standards

Stage Three: Organizational Development and Maintenance

At this stage, the business owner is seeking to institutionalize the business as a way of maintaining business success. The decision facing owners at this stage is whether to leverage the company's accomplishments and expand or keep the company stable and profitable. Therefore, driven by the challenges of increasing business resources and complexity, the business owner or manager realizes it is time to invest in developing the company itself.

The SME continues to struggle as the internal structures, policies, and procedures still bear a striking resemblance to what they were when the company was smaller. This creates some inconsistencies within the organization. For example, employees' roles may not be aligned to their qualifications, incentive systems may not correlate with the company's performance, and policies are not always followed.

Having accurate, up-to-date financial records will be especially important at this stage, since the business owner could be sharing this data with potential investors, shareholders, or other interested parties as he seeks to raise funds to maintain or expand the business operations. Expansion is, of course, optional, based on whether the business owner is happy with the level at which the business is currently operating.

This stage requires strong entrepreneurial skills (which fueled the company from inception), as well as good management and administrative skills. This is the time when the owner begins to realize that he or she can no longer run, control, and manage the entire business operations. This realization could also come in stage two.

There is now an organizational development agenda, and effort is made to professionalize or formalize the structures and processes. As this new agenda evolves, effort is also being made to search for professional managers and specialized expertise, as well as formalizing the internal control systems. Human resources management becomes a strategic imperative to optimize organizational structure and policies.

People-management issues are likely to emerge and become sticky. I have seen situations where hiring new professional managers leads to conflicts between the old and new teams, which often affect employee morale and motivation. This also places the founder in a dilemma: one cannot exactly fire the old staff, but you cannot afford to have them undermine the newly hired professional managers or sabotage their efforts. As the business begins to operate less on personal relationships and more on defined policies and procedures, some may find the transition difficult. Business owners and management need to pay attention to boosting company culture and inspiring employees.

Potential Governance Challenges

- operational inefficiencies as the business struggle to formalize its processes and policies
- decentralization and delegation can become unstable or unclear with new hires
- new vs. old staff dichotomy could create conflict
- poor corporate planning and execution
- inconsistent budget
- frequent power shifts or changes in key management positions
- lack of controls and accountability and an excessive focus on process

Suggested Corporate Governance Stance at the Maintenance and Organizational Development Stage

With the need for external funding comes greater attention to pulling together the elements of a functioning governance system. During this stage, corporate governance structures should be clearly established and practices formalized. These practices should support enhanced performance and improved operational efficiency. Control practices must be mature and effective at this stage to strengthen the required efficiency even more so than in previous stages.

It is important to consider the following corporate governance practices (leveraging the governance practices instituted in the previous stages):

- hire professionals for core operational and management positions.
- continue to refine the organization chart, key policies, and statements of fundamental business principles established.
- develop and document strategic plans and budgets.
- consider a functional/formal board (start small).
- establish a clear division of responsibilities and authorities between management and the board of directors.
- increase delegation (must be supported by improved internal controls).
- establish the internal audit function or as an outsource function.
- present necessary performance reports to external advisers or stakeholders..

Stage Four: Business Expansion. Moving On and Up

The business continues to grow, but growth and changes are less rapid and easier to contend with. In this stage, the key problem is how to finance growth and business expansion. Therefore, the business seeks to diversify with the goal of increasing revenue and gaining access to new markets or creating new products.

Having instituted formal (or almost formal) systems and processes, good administration, and professional management (in stage three), the business could be said to be on autopilot (but not quite). While stage three focused on improving management, in stage four, the emphasis should be more on more formal governance, particularly if the founder is at the stage or age where he or she wants to get out of an active management role for personal or business reasons, such as to start a new company, to hire a professional CEO to manage further business expansion, or to pass the baton to the next generation.

I have seen organizations in stage four struggle with creating a balance between the entrepreneurial skills of the founder and the administration skills of the professional managers. This portends danger for the SME. Too much administration, with decision-making concentrated on processes and not on growth, runs the risk of bureaucracy.

When managing a business in this stage, certain challenges related with having more employees, more expenses, and a lot less flexibility than the early days arise. The business owner/manager should conduct a thorough review of the business to identify any operational inefficiencies that could be hurting the bottom line. Business processes should be streamlined as much as possible to keep everything running smoothly.

Potential Governance Challenges

- the management team could comprise of "stooges," with control still resting with founders and family members
- inability to keep employees motivated (and happy!)
- greater operational challenges
- less agility, leading to slow, bureaucratic processes.
- the potential loss of momentum and creativity—the focus is more internal than on the market
- decreased sales due to failure to innovate

Suggested corporate governance stance at the Business Expansion stage

In this stage of business expansion, SMEs begin to take on a semblance of large companies in business structures, management, and governance practices. The decision-making style within the organization can be defined as institutional, and companies enter the territory covered by the traditional connotation of "corporate governance."

Governance practices need to be strong to ensure business continuity and not to embark on any ill-conceived adventure. Effective risk department, strong control environment, readiness to deal with future adventure, and process integration are all required to achieve goals and governance principles, which are related to responsibility, accountability, and transparency.

It is important to consider the following corporate governance practices (leveraging the governance practices instituted in the previous stages):

- initiate documentation of core governance processes
- establish a formal board with appropriate committee structures.
- develop governance code, charters, and policies.
- develop formal HR policies to attract, retain, and motivate employees.
- initiate a succession-planning framework for critical persons.
- ensure the external auditor examines internal controls in the conduct of the audit.
- formally adopt written governance policies, such as code of ethics/ code of conduct, whistleblowing cg code with E&S considerations; succession plan; HR/grievance mechanism).

Stage Five: Sustainability. Staying on Track

A company in stage five has the staff and financial resources to engage in detailed operational and strategic planning. The greatest concerns of the owner and managers of the company will be to consolidate and control the financial gains and to retain the advantages of small size, including flexibility of response and the entrepreneurial spirit. The business owner and managers must professionalize the company by using of tools such as strategic planning and advanced control frameworks, without losing its entrepreneurial qualities.

Management is expected to be professional and decentralized, with extensive and well-developed systems and management infrastructure. The owner and the business are quite separate, both financially and operationally. As the business evolves, it is important to have a futuristic view. A formal board with external independent directors – with no affiliation to management – may also be introduced, as the future needs to be thought through as professionally as possible. These external parties could be representatives of private equity (PE) and venture capital (VC) firms

When representatives of private equity (PE) and venture capital (VC) firms join SME boards, they tend to fulfil both a monitoring and a value-adding role. They may bring expertise that fills a skills gap on the board. Third-party independent directors can play an important role not only in providing expertise, but also in helping to avoid conflict between the entrepreneur and the investors. The future can be sustained by the family if effort has been made over time to professionalize the involvement of the family.

The company has now reached its peak and has the advantages of size, financial resources, and managerial talent. If it can preserve its entrepreneurial spirit, it will be a formidable force in the market. If not, it may ossify. Staying on track is about identifying what the organization needs to stay in business and creating value in the short, medium, and long term. This is the aim of most founders and owners of businesses. It also involves having the appropriate systems and structures in place to protect and maintain the things that enable the actualization of long-term strategies.

Potential Governance Challenges

- lack of skills to consolidate and control the financial gains
- the potential loss of entrepreneurial spirit
- potential inefficiencies due to rapid growth
- sibling rivalry
- succession problems
- the potential tension between the entrepreneur and investors

Suggested corporate governance stance at the Sustainability stage

The business owner may be considering an initial public offer (IPO) in order to raise long-term, patient funds to finance future expansions. The corporate governance framework should mirror that of large companies.

It is important to consider the following corporate governance practices (leveraging the governance practices instituted in the previous stages):

- separate roles of chairman and chief executive officer
- an active board with an appropriate mix of independence, skills, and experience
- a board induction and regular training, including training on relevant industry E&S issues
- a board performance evaluation process and regular review of its composition
- enhanced risk-management processes: board approves risk, routinely monitors risk management and compliance with policies and procedures

Chapter Summary: Points to Pause and Ponder

- Small business is synonymous to visions of big things—such as big ideas, big plans, big revenue, big growth, and big presence.
- Typically, small businesses transition through five stages of development or growth trajectories. At each stage, there are common experiences that provide valuable insights on what works and what doesn't.
- In stage one, the business conception or startup, business owners conceptualize the big idea, testing the market to determine what products and services they need to deploy to become a viable company.
- In stage two, the active growth or ramp-up of the business, companies have demonstrated that there is demand for their product or service and believe that they have a viable business models that can compete within the greater market.
- In stage three, which is the maintenance and organizational development era, companies have ambitions for further growth and development. This ambition takes into consideration the need for the business to stay profitable. Its talent pool is being developed.
- In stage four, the business expansion and moving on and up, companies that have the intent to take the business to the next

level do so while addressing two relevant issues of delegation and cash management.

- In stage five, the company is focused on sustainability, or staying on track. Companies in this stage can often boast of decentralized management and developed systems. The owner and the business are now comfortably apart from each other, and the business has reached a stage where it has financial resources and executive talent.
- The stages are dynamic in nature; a company might be in the process of moving from one stage to another or being in between stages.
- Every small business owner should be astute regarding the stages of growth and the valuable insights on what works and what doesn't that these stages provide. It is good to reflect on the following:

    o   What stage is your business in? Can you relate to the challenges discussed here?
    o   Do you have the complement (quality and diversity) of people needed to manage a growing company?
    o   Do you have now, or will you have shortly, the systems in place to handle the needs of a larger, more diversified company?
    o   Do you have the inclination and ability to delegate decision-making to professional managers?
    o   Do you have enough cash and borrowing power along with the inclination to risk everything to pursue rapid growth?

CHAPTER 6

SMES AND THE CORPORATE GOVERNANCE DICHOTOMY

Despite the fundamental role SMEs play in the African economy, these enterprises are not able to operate to their optimum level due to the challenges they face. The question, therefore, is why do some businesses fail to grow while others seem to hit the ground running and never seem to slow down? At some point, some businesses become stuck in a rut and are unable to move successfully from one stage to the other.

Factors That Affect SMEs' Long-Term Growth and Survival

An extensive body of literature is concerned with factors influencing the performance of SMEs.[102] Indeed, several factors contribute to success or failure of any institution, and studies[103] have identified one of the main challenges that SMEs face, which is lack of financial support. Without enough long-term funding, SMEs cannot fully grow and expand their business. These studies further revealed that corporate governance is a factor in the ability of SMEs to access external funding. This was buttressed by a study focused on Nigeria.[104] Key challenges facing SMEs in Nigeria included quality of management, access to finance, and infrastructure.

In a similar study focused on Ghana, there were a number of factors that affect SMEs' ability to grow and develop fully. These factors (which the researchers called bottlenecks), include access to finance, lack of managerial skills, and regulatory compliance.[105]Most research on SMEs present the view that lack of capital is a strong limitation to SME growth;[106] however, one researcher[107] concluded that although SMEs may cite lack of credit as one of the most pressing factors contributing to growth and success, this can be considered a "secondary rather than primary problem." They suggested that "the solutions lie within the business structures" and relate to "disciplined finance management" and "skilled workforce." Another factor that this study revealed is a lack of managerial skills and experience of the owner/manager.

Most of the factors mentioned above are largely within the SME's internal environment and are controllable by the SME's owner and/or managers. In addition, these constraining internal factors can be alleviated by implementing good corporate governance practices. These internal factors are discussed below.

Access to Finance

In developing economies such as those in Africa, it has been established that SMEs are typically more credit constrained than large companies. This reality severely affects their potential for growth.[108] All businesses require financial resources to start trading and to fund growth, therefore, lack of access to finance constrains business growth.

SMEs can be financed from founders' own wealth or by accessing external sources of finance, whether from informal sources such as family and friends or from formal market-based sources such as banks, venture capitalists, and private equity firms. Once businesses are trading, ongoing development can be financed using retained profits. The finance gap is a well-known problem for African entrepreneurs. In a study on SMEs and growth in sub-Saharan Africa, the percentage of SMEs identifying access to finance as their major constraint in South Asia compared to Sub-Saharan Africa was 49.2 percent and 89 percent respectively.[109]

A very low percentage of SMEs can access bank loans[110] as a large proportion of applications for bank credit by SMEs are rejected.[111] This is sometimes due to lending conditions such as collateral, whereby these enterprises are not able to provide immovable assets as collateral due to their small asset base. Researchers[112] have also found that institutional factors (which are considered "controllable by a company") hinder the ability of SMEs to access funding. These factors point to lack of managerial skills, financial management, and disclosure of financial information.

SMEs often complain that the banks' credit processes and requirements are too onerous and burdensome. In addition, bank credit tends to be costly and short-term. These SMEs are yet to come to terms with the fact that the unstructured nature of their business often creates an enormous risk for any lender or financiers.

In-depth studies[113] of five countries (Kenya, Nigeria, Rwanda, South Africa, and Tanzania) between 2010 and 2012 showed that the share of SME lending in the overall loan portfolios of banks varied between 5 and 20 percent. Reasons for this finding vary, but key contributing factors are the structure and size of the economy and the state of SMEs themselves, as well as the opaqueness of business information.[114] Studies have shown that SMEs are financially riskier and more likely to default on credit terms.[115]

Financial Management

Closely linked to the lack of adequate funds is the problem of poor financial management. Small business owners sometimes do not have the discipline to separate business finance from personal finance, particularly in the early stages of the business. It is often said that "profit is an opinion; cash is reality," and cash remains the lifeblood of any business. To maintain enough cash flow, the business owner or a finance professional must stay on top of the business billing, follow up on outstanding invoices, and make sure the numbers are clear to avoid the risk of overspending.

The quality of record-keeping can affect financial management. Businesses that do not keep updated and accurate records and do not use adequate financial controls have a greater chance of failure than firms that do. If the books are a mess, you cannot have a clear picture of what the numbers are. This means it would be difficult to make smart financial decisions that will promote the growth of the business. Equally important is the fact that your financial information will be mostly opaque, to the dissatisfaction of potential investors.

Business Planning

Many businesses start with an idea for a product or service that appears certain to result in commercial success, but ultimately, some of these businesses fail due to lack of a robust business plan. Every business needs a business plan as it grows. Even those businesses that do have a business plan can fail if their plans are unrealistic and not based on accurate information. When a business has a clear direction, the business owner and the employees can accomplish more, and the business can grow faster. Businesses that do not develop specific business plans have a greater chance of failure than businesses that do.

Small businesses should be able to produce business plans that forecast cash-flow requirements, have an operational plan, and demonstrate viability and sustainability to secure debt finance. There is a need for better business planning by small businesses in order to obtain external finance, which is required for growth and expansion. In addition, strategic planning to determine the nature of competition and how to position the business is needed. Choice of the business location needs to be considered carefully to minimize distribution costs, meet demand, and beat the competition. There is also a need to choose the product or service that appeals to customers in order to fully satisfy their needs. Poor business planning, namely, not adjusting the plans as the conditions within the market environment change, leads to failure

Leadership and Managerial Skills

The passion, commitment, and leadership skills of the business owner can have a major impact on how quickly and efficiently a business can scale. This is also true for the capacity and competence of the management team. Businesses managed by people without prior management experience have a greater chance of failure than businesses managed by people with prior management experience.

Managerial competencies are sets of knowledge, skills, behaviors, and attitudes that contribute to personal effectiveness.[116] Managerial competencies are very important to the survival and growth of SMEs. Studies have shown that lack of managerial experience and skills are the main reasons why new small businesses fail.[117] Lack of education and training was found to have reduced management capacity in new businesses in South Africa.[118] This is one of the reasons for the low level of entrepreneurial creation and the high failure rate of new ventures.

Owners and managers of small African businesses need to recognize that their skillsets may not be the best for the business through its different stages. There is evidence that one skillset is needed to start up business and another to ensure that that business is sustainable. Many entrepreneurs lack the skills to create coherent strategies and competitive strengths, attract and retain talented employees, develop adequate controls, and introduce clear reporting relationships. Many small companies fail as their founders are great ideas people but cannot execute a strategy. Founders of companies need to ask themselves the question: "Can I execute my strategy myself?" This is often a difficult question to answer, as it requires candid self-examination and a recognition that the generation of great ideas does not always go hand in hand with great performance. Many entrepreneurs are not happy to accept this fact.

For a business to be successful, the founder needs to identify his or her weaknesses and seek help from others with strengths in areas of weakness. These could be skilled employees, consultants, mentors, or nonexecutive directors.

Networking and Stakeholder Engagement

Networking is very important to both new and established small businesses and can positively impact their performance and access to finance. It has been found that the formation of networks helps entrepreneurs to tap into resources within the external environment successfully.[119]

Networking can be used to reduce information asymmetry in creditor/debtor relationships. In addition, networks increase a company's legitimacy, which in turn positively influences its access to external financing. In the absence of effective market institutions, networks play an important role in spreading knowledge about a firm's existence and its practices. Networks also help a firm learn appropriate behavior and therefore obtain needed support from key stakeholders and the general public. This suggests that networking can positively affect the growth and survival of SMEs.

In most cases globally, networks and clusters contribute to business success and continuity. However, it seems as if the African entrepreneur experiences difficulties in establishing and maintaining business networks and clusters that function effectively.[120] Effective stakeholder engagement is a vital networking approach that enables a small business to constantly maintain its value chain and keep abreast with its relationships. However, most small business owners and managers seem to suffer from the peripheral vision loss, or tunnel vision syndrome. They are too focused on running the business and do not pay adequate attention to understanding and effectively engaging with key stakeholders. A business that is not in tune with its stakeholders is a dying business.

Formal Policies and Procedures

As businesses evolve from stage to stage, there is a need to establish formal policies, processes, and procedures. However, these policies, processes, and procedures must be properly aligned to the need and stage of the business. Small businesses do not always get the alignment right. Too few policies, processes, and procedures can prevent the business from scaling up, as decision-making will be strained. Too many of these policies, processes, and procedures can create inefficiency and bureaucracy. It is important to streamline business operations and documentation to reduce inefficiency while remaining effective and allowing your business to scale more smoothly.

At a focus group session, the issue of formal policies and procedures was being discussed as a difficulty for most SMEs. The discussion indicated more a lack of understanding than a substantive conceptual difficulty. One of the participants tried to explain it to the others, but they were not willing to listen to her. She said, "Clearly defining roles and responsibilities within the business, may be cumbersome at the outset, but it gets easier with practice. ... Also, it is of great benefit to us as business owners as it reduces conflict, creates a clear reporting line, and can even help reduce cost from previously duplicated efforts." This was so aptly described, but other participants, while acknowledging the sense in what she said, insisted that this was a great difficulty.

There was also the point of "too many policies." I challenged the participants on the concept of "too many." Who determines what policies there should be? Who determines the purpose of the policies? Who develops the policies? The participants demonstrated a lack of ownership in the process. Other concerns related to this perceived difficulty was the view, expressed by a participant, that "too many formal policies can entrap the organization," while another participant indicated that perhaps "too many formal policies add bureaucracy to the system and slow down decision-making." Another said, "The need to make everything formal can inhibit entrepreneurial expressions." These perspectives disregard the fact that formal policies and procedures add value and enhance operational efficiency only when done right. Agreeably, it takes work to make business policies, processes and procedures function well, but once they do the business owners will quickly see how these can help the company grow.

Rapid Technology Changes.

Gone are the days when a company's operations revolved around filing cabinets and mountains of paperwork. Today's most successful businesses are humming along with the help of cloud-based technology that helps them to streamline their business processes and operate more efficiently. Investment in technology and keeping up with information technology is increasingly important to businesses of all sizes. Technology plays a crucial role in the development of new SMEs. Technology not only helps in evolving a multipronged strategy but also in maximizing business opportunities. Today, information technology is essential to connect with customers and suppliers, manage communication to various stakeholder groups and maintain a brand positioning.

Unfortunately, technology changes pose a big challenge to the growth of small businesses. Most of these enterprises are not able to adopt new technology due to its high initial and installation costs. In addition, this new technology often does not suit the needs of these enterprises. For instance, a small enterprise located in a rural area cannot reap the full benefits of internet connection due to a lack of rural electrification. Adapting to new technology has also been hampered by the slow rate of economic growth in Africa.

Disenfranchised Employees

No matter how strong the business model is, lack of motivation among employees can really hold the business back. Feedback from unhappy employees of SMEs indicates that some business owner/managers do not have a lot of experience with managing people. When there are no formal governance structures in place, employees tend to depend on the whims of the manager. In addition, there is enormous pressure on employees of small businesses. These employees are expected to wear multiple hats when there are no formal business processes, structures, policies, and procedures. Also, when family involvement in the business appears arbitrary, there is usually a buildup of resentment within the workforce. Investing in creating a positive work environment in which employees feel happy and respected will inspire them to commit to the success of the business.

Other Factors External to the Business

Unarguably, and as pointed out by several researchers, the challenges and problems of SMEs can also be traced to external factors. These factors include unfavorable or inconsistent government policies, multiple taxes and levies, access to modern and reliable infrastructure, unfair competition, marketing problems and non-availability of raw materials locally, and insecurity.[121]

It must be recognized that SMEs do not operate in splendid isolation and are not removed from a constantly changing global business environment. Since SMEs do not exist in a vacuum, they are often intrinsically influenced by cultural, political, and economic dynamics of the country where they reside and do business. The performance of SMEs can therefore be actively influenced by systemic factors (external factors). Systemic factors include contractual and informational frameworks, macroeconomic environment, social factors (crime, corruption, and ethics), technology, and the regulatory environment.

The quality of infrastructure affects the growth prospects of SMEs in Africa. Many African countries suffer from a deplorable state of basic infrastructure, such as transportation, telecommunication, and electricity. Electricity supply in some of these countries, including Nigeria, South

Africa, Ghana, and Kenya, does not meet the demand, leading to power cuts, which can affect the production and turnover of SMEs. These external factors are largely outside the control of SMEs.

The Case of ABC Group Ltd

ABC Group Ltd (a pseudonym) is a medium-sized business comprising six subsidiaries based in three West African countries. The structure of the group was evolving at the time, with its main shareholder being the founder/owner/CEO. The company's activities span nutritional food commodities production, distribution, trade, and cold chain storage and management, with emphasis on poultry and seafood. In a conversation with the owner and some management staff of ABC Group, the importance of corporate governance was reaffirmed.

The company was in dire need of funds for its expansion aspirations. The management and staff of the companies within ABC Group recognized the fact that to achieve the goal of expansion in the foreseeable future, there needed to be an almost urgent injection of funds. However, it also became clear that any desire to obtain external funding would be predicated on the adoption of good (or better) corporate governance practices.

The owner was emphatic about his motivation to improve corporate governance, which stemmed from the desire to "seek for and obtain funding from interested investors to grow and expand his business." He also expressed the business need for formalized and improved decision-making processes. Further, in the course of the discussion, he mentioned that he had realized his problem with recruitment and retention of "quality individuals" and that the ability to "increase efficiency at the operational level" might be linked to informal business processes. The owner admitted that most policies and processes, departments, and role definitions were ad hoc and informal in most of the subsidiaries, particularly those in countries where certain regulatory guidelines were not in full enforcement.

He expressed frustration that he had to make all decisions because he did not "have good people." Incidentally, there was clearly very little knowledge, and less understanding, of corporate governance among the companies' executive. The boards in the subsidiary companies were mere boards on paper, without any actual decision-making powers. The legal requirements in the three countries was for SMEs to have a board of a minimum of two persons; however, while this was complied with in all the companies, these were nonfunctional boards. The companies held board meetings to meet specific regulations, but these were not effective decision-making mechanisms.

There was also the challenge with the owner not allowing the established governance bodies to function effectively as he was in control of everything. The owner was heavily involved in the operational business of the company, and the business was heavily dependent on him (presenting a 'key-man' risk). Commendably, the owner had taken significant steps in the direction of creating a "professional" management team, with the appointment of some key managers to the top executive team. However, this team did not make any decision, and as stated earlier, the owner said he did not "have good people."

This business owner had come to a crossroads, which many SME owners arrive at as their business grows and expands. Unlike most SMEs, he had deciphered the source of his problem because the various fundraising efforts had thrown up the lapses in corporate governance. His problem was compounded by the fact that in addition to the obvious need to develop and empower a functioning decision-making body, he also needed to strengthen internal controls mechanisms to prevent fraud and potential losses.

Following a series of conversations with this frustrated friend, I isolated four key issues that he needed to address:

- recruit and retain quality individuals
- formalize and improve the management and decision-making tools by establishing a functioning board and management team
- establish a coherent framework of internal controls appropriate for the business.

It was necessary to translate the needs of the owner and the business into a corporate governance solution. While this seemed like a tall order and an extensive list of matters that needed to be accomplished, it all had to be done in relatively quick succession. These corporate governance actions resonated with other members of the 'board' and executive management because discussions at different levels within the company affirmed and validated the importance of being able to accomplish the item on this list, as it would help the company to scale its biggest strategic huddle—access to finance *("seek for and obtain funding from interested investors to grow and expand the business")*. The second and third benefits expected were to "increase efficiency at the operational level" and "prevent fraud and potential losses." I made an effort to provide constructive feedback to the business owner on the areas where he and his team needed to make deliberate changes in the business to attract the funding required for business expansion.

If the owners and managers of ABC Group had paid attention to corporate governance matters as the business grew over the years, it would have been relatively easy to accomplish their strategic goal. Two years after these initial conversations, my friend was still not able to raise funds as quickly as might have been possible with appropriate governance practices. However, he had made huge strides in improving the corporate governance systems compared to two years earlier, and he was committed to continued improvement.

It has been noted that truly, internal factors (which are considered "controllable by a firm") hinder the ability of SMEs to access funding (which is critical to growth).[122] In other words, most of the constraining factors to SME growth, development, and (ultimately) survival can be alleviated by the establishment of good corporate governance structures and practices at the right time.

At a conference for SMEs in Ghana, a conversation about access to finance ensued. I was delighted that some participants mentioned issues relating to accessibility to funding/capital as a key benefit of corporate governance for SMEs. There was a recognition that banks and financial institutions take corporate governance performance into consideration before making investment decisions. Participants discussed this matter extensively, as one participant enquired, "How do you become a 'loan-worthy' SME?" Another participant opined, "These days, even close friends want to understand your business structures and the quality of your management team before they give you money for business."

One participant complained of his bank's loan-approval process being very slow as the process was cumbersome, with loan officers taking pictures of the inside of people's homes, all in the name of "security," which he said was a result of lack of trust. They concluded that banks and other financial services institutions in Ghana play a predominant role in financing SMEs in the country and that they take corporate governance into account in their decision to put money into a business venture; therefore, if SMEs are able to adopt good corporate governance practices, it will help in attracting finance and investment when needed.

In 2013, the Central Bank of Nigeria established the Micro Small and Medium Enterprises Development Fund (MSMEDF) of N220 billion. Also, a N200 billion Small and Medium Credit Guarantee Scheme (SMECGS) was established by the federal government. In spite of the availability of huge intervention funds aimed at helping SMEs to grow, access to these funds remains a challenge. Apart from the controversies surrounding these facilities, many of the SMEs were not able to access the funds due to the "informal" and "unstructured" mode of business operations.[123] Corporate governance weaknesses seem to be a stumbling block to most SME's ability to obtain financing for their business.

Indeed, CG structures are frameworks to help organizations achieve long-term success, and this is relevant to organizations of all sizes. "Nonetheless, the aims and nature of the corporate governance framework applied to large companies should vary from a framework that can or should be applied to an SME" (ACCA 2015). It has been suggested by practitioners that corporate governance for SMEs should mainly be about improving business efficiency and performance and less about monitoring the actions of management. But, how does one improve business efficiency and performance without monitoring the actions of management?

The business environment in Africa is changing fast, and small businesses, in particular, need to embrace systems that allow them to prosper and survive the test of time. Business owners and managers cannot continue operating with a small-shop mentality and hope to grow. It is a gradual and challenging process to build businesses and develop systems that allow them to run with little supervision by the owner, but it needs to happen. Management and governance systems do not have to be expensive, just functional. SMEs should approach them positively and with a sense of their inevitability.

Debatable Application of CG to SMEs

There has always been a debate about the appropriateness of corporate governance requirements for small businesses. This is because the concept of corporate governance is sometimes perceived to be only relevant for large "corporate" institutions.[124] This perception has led to a lack of emphasis on the need to adopt effective corporate governance practices that could promote good performance for SMEs. However, it is becoming clear that corporate governance does not only apply to large listed companies but also to small- and medium-sized companies that are unlisted.

Traditionally, corporate governance issues arose from the roles of agency and stewardship. Agency involves the transfer of capital from the shareowners to the control of managers. Stewardship refers to the directors' role as guardians of the company's assets.[125] The shareowners, through the board, delegate authority to management and entrust the board to act on their behalf. These roles are, however, important and are more critical when a company's owners (the shareholders) are different from its managers. Therefore, some doubt the applicability of these definitions and descriptions of corporate governance to small companies, where ownership and management and board leadership reside in one person or a small group of people.

Some researchers[126] and practitioners have continued to argue that because the agency arrangement is not very pronounced in typical SMEs, there is no real need for corporate governance structures for SMEs.[127] While this might be a logical stance, studies have uncovered the fact that most of the issues that prohibit access to finance, sustained performance, attraction of qualified personnel and consequently long-term growth in small businesses can be dealt with through the adoption of good governance practices.

I have discovered from practical personal experience that small businesses in Africa appear to be constantly seeking, but failing to access, finance to grow or expand their business ventures. This was one of the factors that my friend (described in the preface) mentioned could potentially derail her dream. This was the main driver for the conversation with the owner and chief executive officer of ABC Group Ltd, described above.

The Business Case for SME Governance

While it may seem obvious that corporate governance is not the only issue/barrier facing small business growth, and while there could be other issues around institutional development in some countries—lack of education, limited access to markets, lack of infrastructure, and other such macro factors—there is still a case to be made for corporate governance.

The business case for corporate governance for SMEs theoretically explores the importance of good corporate governance practices and adoption of good corporate governance principles in small businesses. It also considers how these will affect the performance, profitability and, survival of the small business. It is often appealing (particularly to SME owners and managers) to believe that corporate governance principles do not apply to SMEs since the agency problems are less likely to exist.

However, corporate governance principles are as relevant for SMEs as they are for larger companies to facilitate growth and competitiveness. A strong control system prevents business losses, which could easily erode capital invested. Transparency contributes to a small business's ability to attract financing from banks and other lenders. Proper decision-making and strategic oversight provide the necessary stimulus for a thriving business.

A development institution that works with SMEs to help them improve their corporate governance practices, conducted a study during the two-year period following their interventions. The study found that the changes SMEs made tended to improve performance. For example, they often include the establishment of clearer roles and responsibilities, the strengthening of control systems and succession planning activity. These findings are in conjunction with more easily quantifiable data, such as additional finance raised by the SMEs.

Various research studies conducted in the last two decades indicate that SMEs can gain a range of benefits from establishing appropriate corporate governance practices in their businesses. These benefits include:

  … better overall decision-making and strategic oversight

  … less risk of conflict between family members or other owners who are actively managing the business and those who are not

  … enhanced access to external funding for growth and expansion

> … access to professional managers (beyond family members), external advice, and wider networks
> … faster business growth
> … greater resilience to fraud, theft or other financial costs due to poor internal controls.
> … sustainability and proper management of succession

In a competitive, globalized world, corporate governance has been proposed as a strategy to invigorate the competitiveness of small businesses. It has also been discovered that the ability of SMEs to introduce strategic change is often dependent on the functionality of the corporate governance mechanisms.

Despite these benefits, SMEs still find reasons for inaction. One reason that I have heard quite often is the viewpoint that if corporate governance is such a great idea, companies in developed economies ought not to fail, as they are the proponents of good corporate governance standards and practices. This raises questions about the "form versus substance" of corporate governance adoption—the box-ticking exercise versus real commitment to implement corporate governance. This distinction makes a huge difference to the benefits that can be derived from corporate governance adoption.

Governance: Not a One-Size-Fits-All

When it comes to providing guidance to SMEs on corporate governance, there is no one-size-fits-all approach or solution. SMEs are highly diverse, and this diversity needs to be considered. There are typical challenges and governance-related risks and opportunities associated with each stage of development (*see chapter five*). Therefore, small business owners are encouraged to consider corporate governance in tandem with the business evolution. It is also worthy of note that stagnation and even business decline can happen at any stage and for a variety of reasons, including failure to address governance risks.

Scale is important; therefore, relevance and applicability are critical considerations. Corporate governance structures for small businesses should be set up to enable an effective management of key competencies. It is important to set up specific and simple SME governance arrangements that reflect the form and architecture of small businesses. Small business owners will be less reluctant to adopt corporate governance if they view governance as an evolutionary process, where the systems and processes need to remain fit for purpose as they progress along with the business growth trajectory.

There are various tools to help a small business owner or manager determine the stage of growth for the business. A great tool is the IFC SME Governance Guidebook,[128] which addresses the risks and opportunities faced by SMEs at the various stages of their lifecycles, offering fit-for-purpose and relatable corporate governance perspectives and recommendations. There is also the IFC SME Governance Matrix,[129] which summarizes key governance actions recommended for each stage of SME development.

Unfortunately, SMEs are not embracing corporate governance in the majority of African countries. The major reasons that have been given by most SMEs for not adopting or establishing corporate governance structures include the following:[130]

- Unsuitability to smaller businesses (a small-scale eatery or a grains supplier may not need a board to make viable business decisions. Similarly, the strategic and oversight needs of a one-year-old, five-person business are different from a ten-year-old, sixty-person production company.)
- Concerns that involving others in the running of the business or extensive disclosure of business information means "letting go" of control or losing autonomy, which is typically unacceptable to many African SME owners.
- The costs of establishing and implementing corporate governance structures are considered too high as compared to its benefits. Also, it is often seen to be an unnecessary additional cost to business, considering the dearth of financing. Besides, there are no guarantees that the SME will benefit from cost savings as a result of raising corporate governance standards in the business. Affirmatively, there is a cost associated with implementing corporate governance (e.g., appointment of independent directors, developing internal control systems and external audits). However, these costs are outweighed by the medium- to long-term benefits. A

potential investor seeing that the foundations for good governance already exist will have more confidence in investing or giving loan to the business.

- There is generally a lack of awareness among SMEs regarding corporate governance and its relationships with corporate performance. Across Africa, most countries are in the process of developing codes of corporate governance or revising old versions of their code. This means that even the larger firms have only recently been encouraged to adopt corporate governance. It will take some time before the benefits of adopting it will emerge to encourage small businesses to embrace it.

What Do Small Businesses Really Need?

The term "governance" in its original form implies how something is run or controlled. It could be argued that governance exists in every company. The problem is whether it is good or bad governance. Owners and managers of small businesses should view governance practices as a means to an end and not the end in itself. It is often said that governance is a journey, not a destination. It should be applied to help small businesses perform effectively and be sustainable in the long term.

I was involved in a series of corporate governance workshops that were designed and conducted specifically for SMEs across four African countries—Nigeria, Ghana, Liberia, and Sierra Leone. The purpose of these workshops included raising awareness on the principles and best practices of corporate governance and to provide participants with practical guidance that will allow them to identify priority governance changes most beneficial for their specific companies.

While the workshop was geared towards helping SMEs to understand the basic concept of corporate governance and how it applies to their scale of business, it also enabled an assessment of the level of conceptual understanding, and the issues considered important to these SMEs. It helped to establish what role corporate governance can play in the development and long-term viability of these small businesses in Africa. During one of the group exercises, the SMEs were required to note (on a flipchart) the areas where they needed more help and guidance. The three most prevalent responses were as follows:

1. Succession planning
2. Attracting finance
3. Managing people

These responses reflected the needs of the SMEs and points to the fact that as SMEs, they were concerned about the sustainability of the business, worried about passing on a viable business to the next generation, and worried about how to ensure business continuity in the event that they were absent or indisposed (which reflects their need for credible business managers). The concern about attracting finance is characteristic for most small business owners. These concerns align with the factors enumerated, and described, above that affect SMEs' long-term growth and survival

Therefore, adopting appropriate corporate governance structures should place small businesses in good stead to obtain what they really want.

Chapter Summary: Points to Pause and Ponder

- A small business can develop into a large company, graduating beyond the SME sector. Alternatively, the small business could fail to survive and experience an early demise.
- Small businesses fail for a plethora of reasons. There are both internal and external factors responsible for small business failures.
- One of the main challenges that small businesses face is lack of financial support, because without sufficient long-term funding, small businesses cannot fully grow their business.
- Although SMEs may cite lack of credit as one of the most pressing factors contributing to growth and success, this can be considered a "secondary rather than primary problem." Studies have shown that corporate governance is a key factor in the ability of small businesses to access external funding.
- There has always been a debate as to whether corporate governance practices are appropriate for SMEs since the ownership, board leadership, and management tend to reside in one person or a small group of people.

- Good corporate governance practices have been proven to add enormous value to large corporate organizations, which small businesses can learn from.
- The major reasons that have been given by most SMEs for not adopting or establishing corporate governance structures include unsuitability, potential loss of control, and cost.
- Good corporate governance is a means to an end and not an end in itself; governance is a journey, not a destination.
- The pertinent needs of small businesses include access to finance, succession management, and people management. Good corporate governance practices deliver on these.

CHAPTER 7

GAINS AND PAINS OF GOVERNANCE ADOPTION

A review of corporate governance literature suggests there are a range of factors that encourage or hinder a company's efforts to successfully adopt good corporate governance practices. Factors that encourage adoption of corporate governance are commonly the benefits ascribed to corporate governance implementation or the business case for corporate governance. While factors that hinder adoption of corporate governance are the difficulties that small businesses could face in trying to implement corporate governance changes.

To promote the adoption of good corporate governance by small businesses, it is important to understand the perspectives of small business owners and managers. We must understand their perspectives with the aim of establishing which elements of corporate governance contribute to business performance and which are most difficult to implement.

Gains of Governance Adoption

A participant at a workshop organized in Kenya made an insightful comment. "The gains to be had from incorporating corporate governance in any business (no matter its size) are not commonly known and as such not appreciated or widely sought after by entrepreneurs in this climate."

Corporate governance practitioners promulgate the notion that corporate governance is good for business and adds enormous value. Several studies have established that corporate governance adds value. I conducted a further research study in 2016-2019 to find out (from the perspectives of SMEs in Africa) what specific elements of CG create these benefits of value addition. The proverbial hearing from the horse's mouth.

A typical SME wants to be successful in business to experience profitability and growth. In order to increase the scope of an SME's success, there is need to raise funds to grow and expand its business. There is also the need to have the right people whom the owner can trust to keep business secrets but also to perform well. The top three elements outlined below are those that SMEs identified as enablers of an SME's business vision or goals.

1. Commitment to Corporate Governance

Commitment to corporate governance covers business planning, corporate governance structures/formal policies and procedures, and HR management. This is an important element that SMEs indicated adds value. Commitment to corporate governance is the demonstration of a clear focus on effective structures and processes for achieving the benefits of good corporate governance. In companies where processes and policies are well defined, it commands the same advantages as having a strong management team. It also ensures that roles and responsibilities are well-defined, and actions are being followed through to ensure effective operations within the various departments. Commitment to good corporate governance (as described in chapter 3) involves putting structures, policies, and procedures in place, but beyond this, it should translate to the company's culture of practices and tone at the top.

Commitment to good corporate governance is the behavior and culture that permeates the company and the level of acceptance of the business case for good corporate governance. Formal structures, policies, and procedures are often required as the backbone of any corporate governance framework. A strong commitment tends to have a demonstrable effect on shareholders, potential investors, and stakeholders in the company.

Link to SME performance and value creation. Demonstrating commitment to good corporate governance practice has positive internal and external impact. It signifies to employees that the company can be trusted and similarly to external stakeholders that the company is worth taking seriously. There is a correlation between commitment and entrenchment of corporate governance practices in a company.

An SME owner/manager from Nigeria described a personal experience where the demonstration of a clear understanding of corporate governance and a willingness to embark on a program to enhance the governance structures and practices in her business produced a positive reaction from a potential business partner.

The owner/manager of a medium-sized business in Kenya also shared his experience. In his own words, "once, when we were trying to hire a senior accounts officer, someone who would head our accounts department, we realized that there were some lapses. The preferred candidate asked a few questions which bothered on responsibility, accountability and controls. It was then clear that there were corporate governance practices, which we had not paid attention to. The candidate didn't join the company, but that process helped us figure out a few things and make changes."

2. The Board of Directors and Management Team (Decision-Making Bodies)

The establishment of management teams was a key contributor to value for SMEs. This was mainly because this contributed to good decision-making for the company and invariably supported development and growth for SMEs. Having a strong management team also indicates to external parties that the company is serious about making business progress. There will be better planning, improved sales and marketing practices, and overall operational stability.

There was a consensus on the fact that a strong and professional management team is important to "help the business to move forward and be profitable." This has growth implications. In addition, having a strong and diverse management team helps to contribute to good business decisions, which will reflect on the company's growth trajectory.

Link to SME performance and value creation. While traditional corporate governance frameworks place the emphasis on the board of directors as the main organ of decision-making, it was discovered that a strong management team adds better value to small businesses than a board. A strong corporate governance process would normally cover the decision-making, managerial, and organizational processes they imply and how relevant these are to the business model.[131]

3. Control System and Processes (Internal Control / Internal Audit)

The institution of internal controls contributes to the reduction of fraud, pilferages, and other control lapses in an organization (as there will be structures and processes). This adds value to the company's profitability. SMEs felt that this was an area where the company could reduce potential losses, and for most SMEs at the focus group sessions, any mechanism that could reduce or limit operational and financial losses was very valuable to an average SME. While there was not much debate on this element, it appeared that the SMEs did not have a grasp of the concept of strong internal controls, but to the extent that it could help reduce fraud or control "laxity in expenses," there was an acceptance that it was important.

Link to SME performance and value creation. In a research study[132], it was rightly concluded that SMEs are vulnerable to fraud due to internal control lapses by employees and incur significant losses as a result. The perspective shared by some SMEs indicated that SMEs see fixing internal control and internal audit gaps as a way to avoid losing money, which adds to the bottom line.

Internal control is described as "a set of mechanisms designed in order to motivate individuals to attain desired objectives."[133] Research has shown that internal control and fraud prevention actions are critical for SMEs and could have an influence on SMEs performance.[134]

Unrecognized Gains

While one can articulate the areas that are important to SMEs, which act as enhancers of business performance and motivation for corporate governance adoption, the areas that have been excluded would need to be considered. These could be described as unrecognized gains, since SMEs did not perceive their relative importance to business success.

Succession Planning

The rate of demise in the SME sector in Africa is higher than in other emerging economies. SMEs in Africa seldom succeed to the second and third generations. Therefore, succession should be important to SMEs, but there is very little understanding of the process or relevance of such a process. While most SMEs acknowledge that they want a business that can be left as a legacy for the next generation, there is a degree of reluctance to broach the subject too deeply. In Africa, people generally believe that you do not speak about death or call forth 'evil'. For most people, any discussion of succession tends to evoke a sense of dying or being incapacitated. None of these options appeal to SME owners. Interestingly, external managers of small businesses consider this element as critical to value addition.

Establishment of a Formal Board of Directors

While having a management team is adjudged to be value adding, having a board does not seem to be an important aspect of corporate governance for SMEs. Traditionally, boards of directors are governance bodies that serve important functions for organizations, ranging from monitoring management on behalf of shareholders to providing strategic resources.[135]

While this may be a laudable role to play, SMEs do not apparently perceive value from having a formal board. This is important for policymakers and financiers because it means that while policymakers and providers of funds require a board, it would only amount to a board on paper, without responsibilities or power of influence on the business (i.e., no real value). Instead, it could be worthwhile to pay more attention to the management team and ensure that it is strong and able to deliver performance results. From practical experience, an advisory board may also provide more value for SMEs than a full corporate board of directors. The fact of independence is also a red herring for the SMEs, particularly as the pool of SMEs in Africa comprises predominantly family-owned/ managed businesses.

Challenges experienced with the establishment of a formal board of directors stem from the need for independence as expected by good corporate governance principles. There was not much independence in the composition of either the board or the management team in the SMEs interviewed. An interviewee said, "Our board is made up of family members, no external person. Based on the corporate governance mandate, I guess it is good to have outsiders on the board, but we are not there yet. There are a few outsiders on the management team though." Another interviewee opined, "We … do not like to open up ourselves for fear of being taken advantage of." This mindset affects the likelihood of inviting outsider onto the board.

Having a board provide checks and balances doesn't necessarily mean slowing down growth or innovation. Strong boards challenge founders, make important introductions, partner in growth, and ultimately make a company more sustainable for the long term.

External Auditors

Another interesting part of the control system and processes is the audit of financial statements by external auditors. Most SMEs have external auditors by compulsion, and there may be a need to review what benefits external auditors provide to small businesses. There are certain characteristics that imply that external auditors may not be adding as much value as policymakers and providers of funds require.

- Instances of external auditor serving the company from "inception," which sometimes meant ten to twenty years. This compromises the independence, objectivity, and professionalism of the auditor.
- Appointment of external auditors on the whim of the owner or CEO, who is probably a friend of the auditor, reeks of ineffectiveness and lack of objectivity.
- External auditors performing several roles—bookkeeping, tax consultant, strategy adviser, etc—compromises the quality expected from the external audit firm and its partners.

Therefore, SMEs do not always perceive or expect value from the act of external auditing. Interestingly as I conclude this section, the President of the Federal Republic of Nigerian recently signed into law a revised Companies and Allied Matters Act (CAMA 2020), introducing new provisions to promote ease of doing business. One of these new provisions is the exemption of small companies or any company having a single shareholder from the requirement to appoint an external auditor.

Transparency and Disclosure

While the concept of transparency and disclosure is seemingly important, most SMEs express reluctance to disclose in a transparent manner. There was a sense that the business *'secrets'* must be well kept. There was concern about taxes being imposed on the business if results are publicly shared. There was also the concern of increased regulatory scrutiny and pressure. Aversion to transparency and disclosure "may be due to various reasons, ranging from the reluctance to reveal critical information to competitors to non-transparent practices to minimize the tax burden."[136]

Research[137] points out that the decision of a bank to lend to an SME would inevitably be based on adequate and systematic disclosure of information on SME finance and governance (including the availability of a strong SME business plan). Unfortunately, information disclosure and business planning have been among the major weaknesses of many SMEs (see chapter six).

Family Business Governance

Family business governance is an important topic for discussion to establish a formidable family ownership and control. Family business governance is really a means of formalizing the interaction between the business and the family, to achieve the goals of both without jeopardizing either. In a research[138] in another emerging market—Taiwan—it was concluded that "the influence of family ownership on SME performance is positive and significant" and there is no reason not to achieve this for SMEs in African. Not paying due attention to the interaction between the family and the business often creates conflict (see chapter eleven).

Pains of Governance Adoption

In order to promote corporate governance adoption among SMEs, it is important to determine the pain points or areas that SMEs have difficulty adopting. The top three elements outlined below are those that SMEs identified as most challenging to adopt.

1. Commitment to Corporate Governance (Business Planning, Corporate Governance Structures/Formal Policies and Procedures, HR Management, Succession)

The difficulty expressed was that of a perceived fear that establishing formal structures would limit the ability of the business to be flexible and agile in responding to the business environment. This concern derived from the lack of capacity to articulate and develop the right structures and policies that would create an enabling environment for the business to thrive. Another problem that this poses for most SMEs is the fact that the business environment changes so rapidly in Africa generally, and as such, there was the notion that perhaps, there is no real need to establish formal policies and structures, however, these provide indication of a well-run institution.

Organizational commitment represents the strong believability of organizational values and goals. There appears to be a general problem for SMEs to balance the need for formal policies and the reality of an informal culture. Based on series of conversations with small business owners, there is an aversion towards formalized structure and policies. Some SMEs feel that formal structures and policies would limit entrepreneurial activities, while others feel it would be too binding for the company. Invariably, SMEs tend to prefer a flexible, informal environment.

Unfortunately, the corporate world is less comfortable with informality; therefore, SMEs need to become better at establishing formal corporate governance structures, policies, and procedures.

2. The Board of Directors and Management Team (Decision-Making Bodies)

"It is difficult to trust other people with your business as they may not be able to manage it very well." This is one of the comments that a participant in a

workshop held in Ethiopia offered as a reason for the problem that SMEs face with establishing strong management teams. Another opined, *"It is very expensive to employ too many senior people in the business."*

One of the difficulties that SMEs face with having a strong management team in place is the challenge of cost. Salaries for highly qualified personnel are not surprisingly high in most countries across Africa. SMEs also expressed the likelihood that these 'so-called professionals' who ask for high salaries may not contribute commensurate value to the business. A comment by an SME owner pointed to the anxiety over cost and value. *"I can't get over the fact that sometimes we can end up paying senior-level employees claiming to be experts, who may not add operational value."*

Another business owner offered a different perspective. *"For me, the pursuit of the bottom line supersedes every other pursuit, although I firmly believe there is so much to be acquired by setting up good corporate governance procedures and mechanisms in my business."* The point was that in pursuing the bottom line, paying high salaries in order to establish a strong management team becomes difficult, although she understood the need. SMEs watch their bottom line with care and trepidation and are very sensitive to any factor that could increase the cost of doing business.

Another interesting comment pointed to the fear of creating a bureaucracy that could potentially slow down business decisions. *"What kind of decision-making body should I put into place without introducing unnecessary bureaucracy in my business?"*

Researches have shown that lack of managerial capabilities and weak management access are the bane of SMEs.[139] This means that most SMEs around the world face similar challenges.

SMEs do not typically employ high-caliber professionals, as they are reluctant to pay top wages due to the size of the business. In addition, SMEs do not usually invest in human capital; there is always the perception that when they incur costs due to training employees, the employees might leave the company, and that would be a loss. These factors contribute to a relatively weak management team and weak employment capacity.

Understandably, SMEs struggle with building a dream team that can support company growth at a low cost.

3. Control Environment (Internal Control, Risk Management, Internal Audit)

Establishing a strong internal control system was recognized as a challenging prospect for most SMEs because of the scarcity of human and financial resources required to do this. In a focus group session in Kenya, a reason was offered for the difficulty faced by SMEs in establishing internal control systems: *"We experience a lot of difficulty in recruiting strong internal control people, maybe because we can't really pay much."*

Due to the prevalence of human and financial resources shortage, *SMEs find it difficult to establish internal control systems*[140]. *According to another participant, "Splitting roles between too many people is not always cost effective."* Two of the key elements of an effective internal control system are the segregation of duties and adherence to processes, policies, and procedures. These are areas where SMEs tend to struggle. The lack or shortage of human and financial resources, as alluded to by one of the participants, makes it difficult to spread work to different individuals.

One of the problems that SMEs face is that they often do not have internal control and internal audit systems or staff.[141] It has been suggested that this is due to cost constraints or lack of understanding of the importance of the function (or both).[142] Studies into this aspect of corporate governance have concluded that in most cases of employee fraud, the internal auditing staff was ineffective or absent or the internal audit system did not exist.[143]

SMEs' struggle with the control environment is predicated on the likelihood that most SME owners have little accounting knowledge and accountants are expected to help in designing and implementing sound internal controls, but this costs money, with which some SMEs are unwilling to part. Based on a study in an emerging market, only 6.8 percent of the SMEs believe that it is necessary to improve their internal control environment.[144]

A participant indicated that his company experiences pilferages in stock, which sometimes go unnoticed for some time due to internal control weaknesses, and his management is working to rectify it. Another shared his greatest problem with internal control activities: "It is difficult to identify the right controls." SMEs need to be able to ensure proper staffing, training, and development and have the right information technology for a strong internal control system. These were some of the challenges that most participants in Nigeria cited as problematic for them in the early to mid-stage of business. According to a Nigerian participant, *"We know that internal control is important to prevent fraud, but it is difficult to formalize all the elements, mainly due to environmental factors here in Nigeria."* Another participant opined on a practice within his company relating to IT systems. "We are not too technologically compliant here, and certain processes are still done manually, but we know that this creates some challenges for staff." Other comments included,

"How do I develop a system of internal controls?"

"What kind of monitoring and oversight are applicable to my own company, and how do I design the right checks and balances?"

Difficulty in establishing and maintaining an effective control environment (internal control, risk management, internal audit) is a real issue for SMEs in Africa.

The Resultant Catch-22 Situation

It is interesting to note that the elements of CG that SMEs suggest could add value to their business were the same areas where they are experiencing the most difficulties with adoption. This presents a dilemma, as it becomes pertinent that SMEs need to build capacity in these areas and policymakers and development institutions need to assist them to enhance performance.

In reflection, it is apparent that SMEs require training and development, policy guidance, and support to address these difficulties. Since SMEs acknowledge that these areas add value to their business, it would be counterproductive to remodel the corporate governance framework. However, it would be important for all (providers of capital, policymakers, and business advisers) to understand that corporate governance for SMEs cannot be a one-size-fits-all. SMEs need to grow and mature into practices that are relevant for their stage of business.

For instance, SMEs that are not highly formalized, regardless of the size and age, should not be expected to go from the point of not having a management team to the point of having a full board. This would amount to a semblance of governance performance with no substance, popularly referred to as merely ticking the box and disregarding the spirit of the concept. Rather, SMEs should be encouraged to explore alternative routes to creating a board, by taking an initial step to either have a strategic (formally appointed) advisor, establishing a strong professional executive team, or constituting an advisory board. These initial steps should help the SME to feel comfortable with progression toward formality

SMEs, on the other hand, also need to change their paradigm and understand the expectations and requirements of potential employees and providers of funds. This means that an SME should not expect to go seeking funds from an institution such as a bank without consideration for the level of formality that is required. They should also understand that every level of formality would need to have a positive track record. This means that an SME with a board of directors or management team that was formed a month ago would be less credible that one formed two years ago. Similarly, robust internal control systems do not perform overnight. There needs to be time to mature and show results.

Ancillary Concerns

As part of my 2019 research, participating SMEs were asked to reflect on what general challenges or hindrances SMEs face that negatively affect their appreciation and adoption of good governance practices. Responses to this question provided valuable insight. These challenges include the following:

Lack of Capacity or Skills to Address Corporate Governance Issues

There was a collective agreement that there is a general lack of knowledge and skills in this area, which calls for education, capacity building, training, and awareness creation. Being able to address corporate governance issues is a pain point for most SMEs, and they need help on how to implement.

Every time I speak to an SME about corporate governance, it starts out like most normal business discussions. There is little interest at the outset. Then, when the benefits of corporate governance to the business success are broached, their eyes often light up, and there is a surge in the level of curiosity and interest. As the discussion progresses, I am met with a glazed look, which typifies confusion and helplessness. This is sometimes followed by a polite question or comment indicating that the concept is great but not so great to implement—especially (I am often told) since the business owner has a thousand and one business activities to deal with. The truth is, SME owners and managers do not really know what to do, how to do it, and when to do it. Most SME owners and managers know why it should be done, yet a majority will throw their hands up in the air in frustration when it gets to the point of application.

The Cost of Corporate Governance

The matter of cost of adopting or implementing good corporate governance practices always comes up as part of discussions on corporate governance for SMEs. There was a point made that the cost of corporate governance makes it difficult to attempt building the necessary structures and policies or capacity to implement. Being able to address corporate governance issues is a pain point for most SMEs, and due to limited financial resources, it is understandable that there is a reluctance to build the capacity necessary to address corporate governance gaps or implement good corporate governance practices.

This issue is considered a hindrance by most SMEs. The economic situation of African countries in the last twelve months, which has affected the purchasing power of the average consumer of goods and services, has had a culminating effect on the cash flow of most SMEs. While SMEs acknowledge that corporate governance is important and they need to be trained to implement new practices, a participant at the focus group session made the comment that training costs money, and a typical SME would rather put money in the business than attend training on corporate governance.

While I can relate with the problem, I often say to SMEs that CG appears to be costly for a variety of reasons.

1. It may not deliver the required benefits immediately or as quickly as the business owner wants. Otherwise, a simple cost-benefit analysis will make it worth the while, and the cost will be adjudged as an investment rather than an expense. However, SMEs need to be patient as the business gets used to new ways of working and will begin to reap the benefits with time.
2. Most SMEs tend to continue their regular activities, refusing to make any attitudinal changes as required to demonstrate an enhanced

commitment and action toward good corporate governance practices. Then they create the semblance of a corporate governance framework as a façade, a mere cover on the old ways of doing things. This creates a problem, becoming an albatross and an expensive one at that. Corporate governance should be an integral part of the business culture and not just independent rules and practices.

Lack of or Weak Corporate Governance Regulations for SMEs

It is also worth emphasizing that corporate governance frameworks and their effectiveness are influenced by the environment in which they exist. In an economy characterized by widespread corruption or weak enforcement of laws and regulations, company action to implement corporate governance standards may be frustrated and have limited impact[145]. Such constraints need to be understood by all.

There was a general feeling, particularly in Nigeria, that regulation has not helped promote corporate governance for SME. While the SMEs did not sound as if they wanted more regulation, they seemed to believe the regulation was not of the right type for SMEs. There was a general sense that the existing rules cater to large companies. SMEs in Ghana complained that business growth is negatively affected by unstable policy climate, incessant regulatory bureaucracy, unfriendly trade regulations, corruption, and excessive tax regimes.

In Nigeria, the complaint was of a similar nature and included unfriendly regulatory interferences, tight monetary and credit policies, a difficult workforce, and onerous labor policies. A significant drawback that SMEs encounter in most African countries is that there seems to be an ineffective system of cooperation between different regulatory authorities and that the low level of coordination of provisions under these laws, decrees, and regulations causes uncertainty (and sometimes, frustration) for SMEs.

There were also concerns about the need to make regulations generally and including corporate governance regulations more "SME-friendly." According to an SME owner/manager in Algeria, an article he read mentioned that some guidance on corporate governance practices for SMEs has suggested a "simplified" version of the corporate governance practices than those recommended for larger companies.

SMEs do not like to think that they will be offered a "simplified" versions. In any case, SMEs do business in the commercial world, which means they will be subject to similar standards of scrutiny. SMEs have unique needs and limitations; therefore, regulation needs to take cognizance of these unique needs and limitations. In Nigeria, the participating SMEs are of the opinion that there should be greater levels of transparency, responsibility, and accountability in regulation, because this will encourage SMEs to make progress towards the adoption of corporate governance.

Interestingly, according to the World Bank's *Ease of Doing Business Report 2019* (the Ease of Doing Business Index ranks countries against each other based on how the regulatory environment is conducive to business operation), the large African economies improved their ranking on the scale, which implies that effort is being made to improve the business environment including regulations.

Chapter Summary: Points to Pause and Ponder

- There are some factors that encourage adoption of corporate governance. These are the benefits ascribed to corporate governance implementation.
- Factors that hinder adoption of corporate governance are the difficulties that small businesses could face in trying to implement corporate governance changes.
- SME owners and managers share their perspectives on elements of corporate governance that are beneficial as well as elements that are difficult to implement.
- Interestingly, the elements of CG that SMEs suggest could add value to their business are the same areas where they are experiencing the most difficulties.
- Providers of capital, policymakers, and business advisers need to understand that corporate governance for SMEs cannot be a one-size-fits-all.
- SMEs need to also change their paradigm and understand the expectations and requirements of potential employees and providers of funds.

- SMEs need to grow and mature into practices that are relevant for their stage of business.
- There are other general challenges or hindrances SMEs face that negatively affect their adoption of good governance practices. These include inapplicability of governance principles/practices, lack of capacity or skills to address CG issues, and lack of or weak governance regulations for SMEs.

SECTION THREE

ASSOCIATED CONCEPTS OF CORPORATE GOVERNANCE FOR SMES

CHAPTER 8

CONSIDERING OTHER STAKEHOLDERS

For SMEs, high-quality relationships with financiers, customers, suppliers, employees, and the local community underpin their value. One of the key elements of corporate governance described in chapter three is *stakeholder engagement*. SMEs must find a simple and structured way to demonstrate a commitment to good corporate governance by engaging strategically with stakeholders. This effort is really an investment in the future.

As part of the 2019 research study, discussions were held with various stakeholder groups in a bid to gain their perspectives on the concept of corporate governance for SMEs and the wider implications.

Employees and Contractors

There is an assumption that a challenge of growth and development experienced by SMEs in Africa is caused by the difficulty in hiring skilled employees who could add value to the company. It has been suggested in the literature that weak corporate governance practices in smaller businesses made it difficult to hire good people.

The *2017 State of Small Business Report* from a survey of more than 1,100 small businesses, presented by Wasp Barcode,[146] indicates that 50 percent of SMEs owners say hiring new employees was one of the top challenges they faced in 2017. A similar report, the *TradeGecko 2018–2019 State of Small Business Global Report*,[147] provides insight to small businesses' answer to the question, "What held you back from growing more?" Hiring the right staff was one of the top three responses received from small businesses.

Recruiting the right people is crucial for any business and presumably more critical for smaller businesses. While this study by Wasp Barcode focused on the United States, it is easy to find a correlation to challenges facing African SMEs. For small businesses, hiring is one of the most important factors that can help the company grow as years succeed to years. Employees are the lifeblood of any organization and are responsible for the long-term business success.

In 2019, small business owners reported a significant 15 percent increase in challenges with recruiting and retaining employees. Many small business owners (about 41 percent) employ only two to five employees, which means each employee counts—underperformance can be deadly to a small business's profitability. Given these small employee populations, recruiting and retaining top talent is understandably a major concern.[148]

Unfortunately, it has been observed that talented and skilled labor is relunctant to work for small businesses. This is because small businesses neither pay well nor offer incentives for career growth nor invest in developing their human resources. As a result, these businesses do not have good management structures and human capital, resulting in lower productivity. Managers in these businesses (even if they are not family members), sometimes lack professional training and are unaware of the importance of corporate governance.

Discussion with a recruiter who delivers service to clients across West Africa provided some insights. Generally, SMEs like to hire by themselves, as they feel it is too expensive to get the services of professional recruiters. However, sometimes the more mature and structured SMEs seek out professional recruitment services. At the time of this discussion, about 20 percent of the recruiter's portfolio was made up of SMEs at different stages of development. Challenges faced when helping SMEs find employees as shared by the recruiter include the points below:

- Most small businesses are not able to project a strong brand and cannot communicate that they are a good/attractive place to work as easily as bigger companies, who have deeper pockets for marketing/advertising. The business environment in West Africa is very competitive, and employees are often seeking for employment in well-known companies.

- Some business owners/managers do not have a lot of experience with managing people. When there are no formal governance structures in place, employees are at the mercy of the whims of the manager.
- SMEs operate relatively lean operations, and often, they require employees to wear multiple hats. This is because of a lack of formal business processes and structures, policies, and procedures. Weak governance arrangements do not augur well for most professionals and tends to put them off.
- SMEs tend to lean on family members to fill important roles in the business. When there are no governance structures in place for hiring family members, employees sometimes are looked over for promotion or feel that inexperienced managers, who are members of the family, are placed to supervise their work. This is demotivating for a lot of people and discourages professionals from looking to SMEs for employment.

Arguably, there are countless challenges facing SMEs with regard to hiring and retaining staff. While better corporate governance practices will certainly not eliminate all the challenges, it would place a small business in good stead while searching for skilled professionals to grow their business.

There is a growing working population in Africa, and SMEs play a role in providing jobs in various sectors of the economy. One of the reasons that small businesses matter is that they have the potential for generating employment. Studies have shown that the labor intensity of the SME sector in Nigeria is much higher than that of the large enterprises.[149] This is consistent with studies in Ghana, which also concluded that the larger companies do not generate as much employment as the SMEs.[150] This perspective is consistent across Africa and other emergent economies.

This means that SMEs in Africa should ideally not have a shortage of managerial skills, but sadly, they do. Poor management skills and practices by SME operators was cited as a reason for the reluctance of financial institutions to extend credits to SMEs.[151] HR consultants and managers have alluded to weak managerial skills and decision-making structures as inhibitors to SMEs' ability to attract and retain employees. Typically, managers have the most direct influence on employees they manage. They have a responsibility for aligning the performance of their employees with the overarching organizational goals and shaping organizational culture.

However, as the rate of unemployment continues to rise in Africa,[152] SMEs should be considered as a panacea. For employees or potential employees of SMEs, it is essential to know what to expect from SMEs. There should be an understanding of the stage of the business that the SME is in before, and during employment, and a clear focus on how this will influence the employment or what flexibility the employee might have to make a change.

Investors and Financiers

"SMEs are of great socio-economic significance although their long-term growth and competitiveness has been compromised by the chronic and often acute constraints on their access to formal-sector finance, among other systemic and institutional problems in developing countries."[153]

Having interacted extensively with financiers of small businesses, including banks (which provide business loans and advisory support to SMEs), venture capital (VC), and private equity (PE) firms, I have learned that these institutions care about how businesses that they invest in are organized. Discussions held with investment and relationship officers of some of these institutions provided some insights on their perspectives regarding corporate governance for SMEs.

Most commercial banks across Africa have SME portfolios and provide mainly short- to medium-term financing to SMEs. These banks tend to have difficulties with SMEs, which impede lending, slow down the process of lending, or increase the attendant cost of lending due to a perceived high risk to the commercial bank. A few of the difficulties shared by some staff of commercial banks (with primary responsibility for SME lending) are as follows:

- SMEs do not often have credible banking history or have a very short bank history, due to their size and the age of the business.
- SMEs do not possess sufficiently valuable collateral to act as security for their borrowing.
- SMEs do not have formal structures in place that would assure a lender of business continuity (succession).
- Inadequate bookkeeping and poor financial management: SMEs do not always have proper books of accounts, and financial statements are not readily available for verification.
- SMEs do not inspire trust due to their informal structures, highly personalized founder-dependent operating model, which suggests a keyman risk.

Some of these issues that affect financing of SMEs can be alleviated by the adoption of a good corporate governance framework, which is appropriate for the size and stage of the business. SMEs are often stranded and have to leverage informal sources of funding (personal funds, funds from family and friends) or resort to very short-term funds (such as overdraft facilities), which the banks can give at high rates of interest. These funding sources, unfortunately, do not provide the needed leverage for growing and expanding a business venture.

There is a financing gap for small businesses in most emerging markets; serious financial constraint is being experienced by most of the small businesses in Africa. In Africa, institutions that typically play a role in the financing of SMEs include commercial and microfinance banks, cooperatives, and other financial institutions (PE and VC firms).

On the other hand, investors are also seeking viable investment opportunities in the region and often look to SMEs. A survey of SME financing in four East African countries, namely Kenya, Tanzania, Uganda and Zambia[154] found that the SME segment is a strategic priority for the banks in the region. SMEs are considered a profitable business prospect and provide an important opportunity for cross-selling. Banks consider that the SME lending market is large, not saturated and with a very positive outlook, although there are several obstacles including SME-related factors.

Undeniably, SMEs that are on the growth and expansion trajectory present a good opportunity for high returns. Africa represents an important investment destination particularly due to its large and increasing population. However, there are some corporate governance issues that an astute investor should be aware of. For example, ownership and governance structures in SMEs involve few shareholders, with strong overlap between owners and management. Invariably, there are close, personal relations between the shareholders, and therefore conflicts can occur due to a breakdown of these personal relations. These factors could culminate in significant economic risk for investors, undermining the viability of an investment.

According to the *World Bank Doing Business Report*, the investor protection index is very low in most African countries, which means that protection for investors in SMEs in Africa is minimal, in addition to other cultural nuances. Investor protection is crucial because, in many African countries, expropriation of minority shareholders (investors) by the controlling shareholders (owners) occurs.

There is still no universal consensus regarding the demand of investors for strong corporate governance processes and procedures. Some investors feel very strongly about ensuring strong corporate governance practices, while there are some who are not very keen and do not mind the "tick box" approach to governance. These investors place a lower value on corporate governance principles and practices and therefore do not demand or insist on them. Some companies that appear very attractive to investors get away with having informal governance structures, processes, and procedures. However, these investors are in the minority.

Investors seeking to invest in SMEs in Africa should realistically take into cognizance the stage of the business. This will help to moderate the expectation of the level of corporate governance practices that the SME can appreciate and adopt. This is because SMEs operate at different stages, and it would be counterproductive to expect all SMEs to adopt all aspects of corporate governance principles in the same way and at the same degree of intensity. As described in chapter 5, SMEs need to grow and mature into practices that are relevant for their stage of business, which means that an investor should realistically expect SMEs to adopt practices relative to their understanding, capacity to implement, and stage of the business.

Possibly both parties should agree on the stage of business, and the practices that are prevalent in that stage. Based on this, there should be an agreement of an action plan or roadmap of actions required to improve CG practices. Effort should be made to understand the elements of CG that SMEs struggle with generally and the elements that the specific SME is struggling with. This would enable investors to manage any risk arising from corporate governance practices or lack thereof. The investors are also able to make an informed decision.

Investors should consider supporting SMEs to build capacity, either by injecting managerial skills in the areas of HR, internal audit, and control, which are the areas that SMEs have great difficulties in adopting corporate governance practices or encouraging training and development.

Clients and Customers

In most emerging market, there is a belief that if there is a good product, customers do not care how a business is structured or what policies and procedures are deployed. Firstly, this begs the question of the likelihood of producing a good product and attracting loyal customers in the absence of good governance practices. Important to mention are the risk of survival, and the reputation of the small business, both of which matter to customers.

One of the reasons small businesses fail is that they fail to understand just how heavily customers determine their success. Customers are the whole reason the small business exists and therefore hold the keys to success in their behavior, values, and satisfaction. In order to stay in touch with customers and understand their wants and needs, small business owners and managers should have formal policies and procedures designed to reach out to, and engage with, their customers.

In the *2017 State of Small Business Report*, growing revenues was fourth on the list of priorities for small business owners. Small businesses say that the top two strategies for improving revenue growth were to (1) improve existing customer experience and retention (2) invest in new customer acquisition activities and methods.

Reputation is very important, and it is often said that it takes twenty years to build a reputation but twenty seconds to destroy it. This is true for individuals (the small business owner) as well as the small business. Again, academic research is informative, demonstrating that the consequences of reputation damage is far-reaching. In this era of social media and online market, the concept of transparency and disclosure is very important. Transparency and disclosure practices create a structured communication between companies and their customers, which enables the customer to better understand the company's products and services.

The way a small business treats and handles the needs of its customers is critical to establishing and maintaining a positive reputation and building a stronger brand. Many businesses might assume the smaller you are, the less your reputation matters. However, that is the farthest thing from the truth. The smaller your businesses, the harder you need to work to build a strong reputation. When businesses are small, they usually sell directly to customers, relying mostly on word of mouth for their marketing needs. Because people buy from people they trust, building customers' trust is as important for large companies as it is for small companies.

Reflecting on the need for formal policies and procedures, these demonstrate commitment to good corporate governance. For example, very few small businesses have a customer care policy. Some small businesses probably think they are too small to have one. But a small business only needs a few guidelines to make a big difference and could suffer dire consequences for a lack of policy. Imagine if the first point of contact at a small business is a gruff, disinterested receptionist who does not even look up when someone comes in or who answers the phone in an off-handed manner?

There must be a company-wide policy to guide employee behavior. This could make the difference in retaining existing customers, selling more to them and attracting new business. It is also about getting more business through referrals and recommendations. All these efforts have bottom-line implications.

Regulators and Policymakers

In 2016, the African Corporate Governance Network (ACGN) partnered with Ernst & Young to conduct a research on the State of Corporate Governance in thirteen African countries, which include Egypt, Ghana, Kenya, Malawi, Mauritius, Mozambique, Nigeria, South Africa, Tanzania, Tunisia, Uganda, Zambia, and Zimbabwe. In reading through the research report, it was clear that in all the countries above, regulation plays a significant role in the state of corporate governance. Most countries in the region are trying to develop new corporate codes or review and revise existing codes. Recent codes have also focused on corporate governance principles without being too prescriptive about the practices, such that these codes will also be applicable to small businesses.

A few countries in the region have specific CG regulations for SMEs. As far back as 2008, the Center for International Private Enterprise (CIPE) supported the Institute of Directors in Zambia to publish a code of corporate governance for SMEs. To assist SMEs with the application of the principles contained in South Africa's *King IV Report*, the report includes a sector supplement to guide SMEs in the application of the principles. Depending on the size of the business, smaller entities may decide to apply the principles of *King IV* on a proportional basis and as their resources allow. For example, while large companies will be expected to have an audit and risk committee, smaller businesses may decide to dedicate a percentage of the time of the governing body to risk management and audit committee related duties or to request one member of the governing body to take responsibility for these duties.

Nigeria's national code of corporate governance for the private sector, public sector, and not-for-profit organizations tried to cover a wide spectrum of business sizes. It, however, specifies that compliance is not mandatory for companies with eight or fewer employees, regardless of status of such companies.

There are enough laws and regulations with respect to corporate governance. However, the major challenge is the absence of active devices for their effective enforcement. Without an effective enforcement of the rules and regulations with regards to corporate governance, it would be very difficult for the region to enjoy the benefits of good corporate governance.

The recommended strategy to ensuring effective enforcement of corporate governance laws and regulations is to recognize that the structure and capacity of the legal and regulatory frameworks are essential components of the corporate governance system. To achieve this, regulators and policymakers need to create effective mechanisms for enforcement as well as strengthen existing enforcement mechanisms, by creating adequate awareness and building capacity. It would be important to encourage the media to report issues of poor corporate governance and become more critical and judicious regarding corporate governance-related incidents.

An important issue is the need to pay close attention to the small business sector and tailor corporate governance guidelines and enforcement mechanisms. Some countries, like Kenya and Nigeria, have already established an alternative stock exchange for small businesses. The Growth Enterprise Market Segments (GEMS) was launched by the Nairobi Securities Exchange (NSE) to provide more options for SME to raise long-term finance. The GEMS provides favorable listing (including corporate governance) requirements that were tailored for SMEs. In Nigeria, it is called the Growth Board, which aims to encourage small- and medium-sized companies with high growth potential to seize the opportunity of raising long term capital and promote liquidity. The Growth Board was established as part of the Nigerian Stock Exchange's initiative for meeting the needs of businesses at every phase of their lifecycle.

To foster the adoption of corporate governance by small companies, regulators and policymakers also require a simultaneous implementation of other strategies, including the gaining of greater access to information, reviewing the current rules and regulations, educating small businesses, and effectively enforcing existing recommendations and guidelines/principles of corporate governance.

Chapter Summary: Points to Pause and Ponder

- Corporate governance promotes effective engagement with business stakeholders, providing relevant policies and procedures to formalize these relationships.
- The challenge of growth and development experienced by SMEs in Africa may be caused by the difficulty in hiring skilled employees who would add value to the company.
- Hiring the right staff was one of the top three responses received from small businesses to the question, "What held you back from growing more?"
- Recruiting the right people is crucial for any business, and presumably more critical for smaller businesses, and underperformance can be deadly to a small business's profitability.

- Adoption of good corporate governance practices gives a small business an edge while searching for skilled professionals to grow their business.
- A critical challenge of small businesses in Africa is the inability to secure funding for business growth and expansion.
- When seeking bank loans, weak corporate governance practices tend to delay lending, slow down the process, or increase the attendant cost of lending due to a perceived high risk to the commercial bank.
- Customers care about the reputation of a small business, and good and appropriate corporate governance practices enhance reputation and brand.

CHAPTER 9
ANOTHER LOOK AT GOVERNANCE PRACTICES

To be applicable and effective, business solutions must be simple. A key to improving the adoption of corporate governance by small businesses is to demystify the concept, making it simple. Typically, proposed solutions to organizational and process challenges have often been IT, HR, or operations intensive, requiring specialized knowledge and complex training or involved the building of complex systems—often lengthy and expensive with uncertain outcomes.

Providing a simplified way to view corporate governance helps small business owners, managers, and employees to be open to the changes required for effective adoption. It is often said that the best solutions are the simplest ones.

A simple way to look at corporate governance is through the lens of the Five-Way Directional model©. The Five-Way Directional model© provides a perspective for leaders to focus their attention in an intentional manner. I first introduced this model at a workshop organized by the European Institute for Advance Studies in Management (EIASM) in Brussels, Belgium, in 2017. It has taken various forms over the years and been used in different contexts and is a useful model for small businesses.

This chapter describes the Five-Way Directional model© and how each aspect of this model must be understood, articulated, and harnessed based on relevant institutional peculiarities, in order to address contextual governance challenges. The Five-Way Directional model© aligns with the key elements of corporate governance described in chapter 3. This model will help business owners and managers to focus their attention in such a manner that they can ease the feeling of the frustration associated with (perceived) corporate governance ineptness.

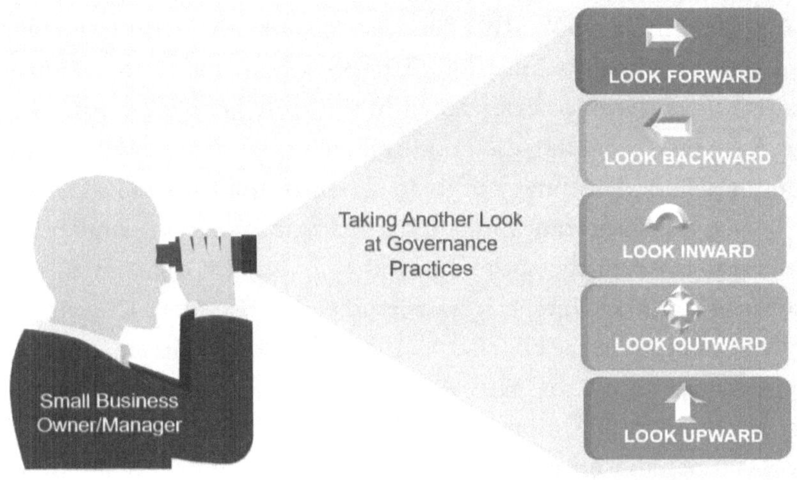

Figure 7 - The Five-Way-Directional model©

A Forward Look (*Strategic Focus*)

In a typical corporate governance framework, the board of directors' mandate to govern a company is a legal responsibility. This mandate, incidentally, is very broad in concept. According to the OECD principles, "The corporate governance framework should ensure the *strategic* guidance of the company, the effective monitoring of management by the board, and the board's accountability to the company and the shareholders."[155]

From the foregoing, the board's duty to oversee the company's business and the long-term strategic plan is one of the most fundamental aspect of a board's role. For a small business, this duty rests on the decision-making body, which comprises the small business owners and managers. Depending on the stage and maturity of the business, this duty could rest on the advisory board or a fully functional board. I spend a lot of time with CEOs and board members of private company startups. My advice to owner/CEOs is that the functional board is a great resource for strategic perspective, and they need to be smart about harnessing the board's experience.

Is the decision-making body, responsible for the direction of your business, looking forward enough? To effectively govern an institution, owners, managers, or directors must look strategically to the future. A strategic plan is a must-have for every small business. It gives the business a real shot at success, providing direction and an impetus for growth. In a small business, where the strategy of the business is more or less in the head of the owner, it is important to share the strategic vison with other members of the team. When the entire business can visualize the company's (and its owners') strategic intent, it is easier to actively support achievement.

Major brands in the US, such as The Body Shop, Walmart, and Subway, started out small in the past. At one point, they also belonged to that relatively obscure but promising group referred to as "small businesses." These companies were able to break out of the league of "small businesses" because of the focused application of business growth strategies. They were able to look into the future and visualize what they wanted to become and then worked tirelessly toward the goal.

The decision-making body should not be composed merely with cronies of the owner, unless they have the right skills, experience and intentions. Typically, the decision-making body should be composed of individuals who are well versed in the complexities of the company and its industry, and can provide the right kind of input to a strategic plan.

To avoid the failure of the small business, the business plan should be realistic and based on credible information and accurate projections for the future. Looking ahead also helps you avoid pitfalls or being caught off guard. Strategy formulation makes it easy to address other matters, such as succession planning. *Failing to plan is planning to fail. Therefore, a forward look is vital for every small business.*

A Backward Look (Retrospective Focus)

A small business owner/manager who has looked forward to develop a viable business plan and established some key strategic goals should be set on the path to success. However, it is important to periodically take a backward look and evaluate the progress that the small business is making toward these goals.

Looking back to move forward is a good business strategy. It helps to take stock of past experiences to gain perspective on future activities. Looking back can also be extremely effective, like using the rearview mirror when driving. While using the rearview mirror is necessary to drive safely, one should not spend too much time looking back. The control system is one of the elements of a good corporate governance framework that can provides historic information about business performance (or lack of performance).

Learning from mistakes (yours and others) is an age-old advice passed down from our parents. While dwelling on the past is not healthy, learning from it can be beneficial. It is understandable to focus primarily on success and suggest improvements to make your future work even more successful, but it is equally important to recognize failures. Studies show that humans learn far more from failure than they do from success. A business leader cannot expect things to change or improve if the business is stuck in the same patterns. Look backward to what was done in the past to get the business where it is now. The information should be used to avoid making the same mistakes repeatedly.

Corporate governance proponents are normally good at asking questions of "what went wrong" after a problem, or when planning for something new. As part of the strategy development process, it is important to look backward retrospectively and become familiar with why some small businesses failed in the past. What did these businesses do wrong? What did they fail to consider? Plan to learn from the mistakes of others to avoid the same disastrous turnout for your business.

The decision-making body needs to have a structured way of looking backward. Information should be shared with shareholders and stakeholders as considered appropriate. Retrospective reviews could be disclosed transparently and demonstrates the agile nature of the small business. Looking backward also helps to identify if there were any control lapses, process failures, or structural gaps to be adjusted. As much as possible, this should be a collective effort.

A *backward look* into the company's origin is also a great way to get inspired about the future direction. A backward look is almost always helpful!

An Inward Look (Introspective Focus)

An inward look is a synonym for internal examination or evaluation. There is a need for the decision-making body of a small business to establish a process for periodic examination of the organization's policies, processes and people. A functional control system is a key element of a good corporate governance framework that can help with such examinations.

Corporate governance professionals always adjudicate for periodic evaluation as this provides a basis for change and continuous improvement. Sir Bryan Nicholson, former chairman of the Financial Reporting Council, UK, said, "Evaluation is essential to improving performance - you cannot begin to address your weaknesses unless you know what they are." How well the small business is performing can be determined by looking inward and comparing the results of initiatives to objectives and evaluating to what extent targets have been met.

Financial indicators can also be used to evaluate small business performance. In evaluating the success of your small business, check how much money it is generating and how it is recorded. Cash is king for most small businesses, and so it is necessary to review the controls around revenue collections and expenditure. The three main financial statements that small businesses can rely on are the income statement, balance sheet, and cash flow statement. The income statement measures the profitability of your business during a certain period by showing your business's profits and losses. The balance sheet shows your business's financial health, measuring how much you owe and own. And the cash flow statement shows how liquid or cash rich your business is. An inward look at the control system and processes can reveal inherent anomalies.

The effectiveness of the company's policies and processes should be evaluated from time to time to ensure that the business is operating optimally. Self-evaluation requires discipline, and for a small business, the discipline of self-evaluation should be embraced not just for the decision-making body but for the operation and the workforce, regardless of size. Often, small business leaders shy away from formal performance evaluation. Evaluation is especially important because the owner tends to become distanced from the everyday running of the business as the business grows.

It is important to evaluate constantly as organizations evolve, and the external environment changes very quickly. It is therefore imperative to ensure that management is sufficiently agile to adapt to changes without losing traction.

After an evaluation, then what? Appropriate action based on the result of the evaluation must be taken. Action may involve enhancing managers with the skills and experience to oversee the risks and opportunities of a transforming industry; or, providing training for employees in areas where a deficiency is revealed.

An inward look reveals what changes are required!

An Outward Look (Systemic Focus)

Looking outward means looking beyond oneself or the business and being cognizant of a broad range of stakeholders. The stakeholder concept is based on two fundamental premises. The first one is that managers need to pay attention to a wide array of stakeholders in order to perform well. The second one is that managers have obligations to stakeholders that extend beyond shareholders. The overarching idea is, therefore, the view that managing or engaging stakeholders is an act of enlightened self-interest.

The *King IV Report* adopts a stakeholder-inclusive approach, meaning that the governing body should take into consideration the "legitimate and reasonable needs, interests and expectations of all material stakeholders in the execution of its duties in the best interests of the organization over time." Stakeholder engagement and management in a small business should be seen as a way of managing risk, increasing sustainability, and improving strategic performance. Good corporate governance is essential to create trust and engagement between companies and their stakeholders, thereby contributing to the long-term success of the business.

Many businesses have come to the realization that stakeholder engagement can improve business performance.[156] The negative consequences of a poor relationship with stakeholders is seen in damaged reputation and poor business performance. It is expected that when a small business engages stakeholders as part of its formal corporate practice, it reaps social performance and goodwill that comes from increased patronage leading to improved market share. Despite the above-mentioned benefits, there appears to be little engagement and cooperation among small businesses in Africa.

Stakeholder management in owner-managed small businesses is rare. When it does happen, the company's stakeholder engagement and management depend on whom the owner/managers perceive to be legitimate stakeholders. The perception of legitimate stakeholders is based on the personal views, exposure, experiences, relationships, and beliefs of the owner/manager. This is somewhat acceptable, as leadership needs to be driving an effective stakeholder engagement. In larger businesses, the board of directors provides inspiration and leadership for stakeholder engagement projects. However, developing and implementing a framework of stakeholder engagement as part of the corporate governance practices for SMEs needs to be a participatory and engaging process. South Africa's *King IV Report* suggests that the SME consider establishing a formal forum where stakeholders can raise questions in order to broaden the concept of stakeholder inclusivity.

Some small businesses are increasingly using digital media to improve their stakeholder engagement. These activities can seem overwhelming for small businesses. However, small businesses need to look outward at their stakeholders and see them as strategic partners to help achieve business goals. When stakeholder engagement is formalized and incorporated into business as usual, there is a greater likelihood that the initiatives and collaboration will add greater value to the business.

An outward look adds great value and ensures sustainability!

An Upward Look (Ethical Focus)

The final dimension is an upward look which depicts an ethical focus. Small business owners/managers must *look upward* and ensure that their responsibilities are delivered with honesty and integrity of purpose.

Business ethics is a process for integrating values such as honesty, trust, transparency, and fairness into policies, practices, and decision-making. Business ethics is, therefore, inherently linked with virtually all aspects of corporate governance. A firm that applies ethical practices also expects to be dealt with ethically. While larger firms have already developed their reputation by formally developing codes of ethics, SMEs are increasingly becoming aware of the importance of codifying good, trusting relationships with customers, employees, suppliers, and the community.

With the efforts against corruption and the intention to promote ethical conduct in their supply chains, larger firms are increasingly asking SMEs (linked to their supply chains) about their ethical policies. However, some small business in Africa are not fully aware or convinced of the importance of business ethics and its advantages. Some important advantages of an *upward look* and the codification and adoption of business ethics include the following:

1. Investors and financiers often use corporate practices and values as primary considerations in their decision-making.
2. As customers are becoming increasingly aware of their rights, they value ethical practices; therefore, adopting ethics can help to build reputation of businesses.
3. Promoting reputation can help in building customer loyalty and increasing revenue.
4. It can help the small business to attract talented workforce and employees as well as improving the dedication and performance of existing employees.
5. Business ethics enhances compliance with regulations (e.g., labor laws and environment). Eliminating the cost of potential regulatory sanctions.
6. It supports collaboration with other firms both domestically and internationally, which can boost business performance.

Due to insufficient resources, SMEs are not able to spend funds on building a *formal* system of business ethics, including codes, training, monitoring and evaluation. However, there are advantages of developing and documenting a formal business ethics policy that will not only create a better enterprise but also increase the moral of its employees.

Chapter Summary: Points to Pause and Ponder

- A forward look is strategic. A strategic plan is a must-have for every small business. It gives the business a real shot at success, providing direction and an impetus for growth.
- The decision-making body should be composed of individuals who are well versed in the complexities of the company and its industry, of finance and financial structure, and of relevant laws and can provide the right kind of input to a strategic plan.
- It is important to periodically take a backward look and evaluate the progress that the small business is making towards its goals.
- Looking back to move forward is a good business strategy. It helps to take stock of past experiences in order to gain perspective on future activities.
- There is a need for the decision-making body of a small business to establish a process for periodic in-house evaluation.
- How well the small business is performing can be determined by looking inward and comparing the results of initiatives to objectives and evaluating to what extent targets have been met.
- Looking outward means looking beyond oneself or the business and being cognizance of a broad range of stakeholders.
- Good corporate governance is essential to create trust and engagement between companies and their stakeholders, thereby contributing to the long-term success of the business.
- Small business owners/managers must *look upward* and ensure that their responsibilities are delivered with honesty and integrity of purpose.

CHAPTER 10

SUSTAINABILITY FOR SMES—A MULTIPLICITY OF CAPITALS

In the last couple of years, large businesses have been talking about multiple types of capitals with relation to sustainability and integrated reporting. Integrated reporting is a generally recognized international framework that helps companies (including SMEs) to better understand and communicate how they create value. The term *capital* refers to anything that increases a business's ability to generate value. These are elements that are needed for a business to deliver its products or services efficiently and effectively.

According to the International Integrated Reporting Framework, also cited in the King IV Report, *"capitals are stocks of value that are inputs to a company's business model and are relied upon by the company for business success. These stocks of value, or inputs, can be increased, decreased, or transformed through the organization's business activities and output."*[157] Featuring this chapter in a book for SMEs raises some questions such as "How do these capitals influence SMEs' success?" "How can SMEs take advantage of these capitals?" "What difference is a multiplicity of capitals likely to make and to whom?"

Initially, a five-capitals model was developed by an organization called the *Forum for the Future*,[158] founded by UK environmental guru Jonathan Porritt. The five capitals are financial capital, manufactured capital, human capital, social and relationship capital, and natural capital. Subsequently, the International Integrated Reporting Council (IIRC) released their model describing six capitals, adding intellectual capital to the initial five. This new model emphasized the strategic focus of an organization, stakeholder relationships, consistency, and comparability, with an enhanced focus on both risk management and corporate governance.

The model on types of capitals is still evolving with new thoughts and perspectives from academia and professionals. I came cross the concept of cultural capital in my study of various literatures on family business, and the African in me could relate to the cultural dimension of business practices and how an understanding of this dimension adds value to small businesses operating in Africa. Adding *cultural capital* to IIRC's list of six capitals, brings the total number of capitals to seven, in my view.

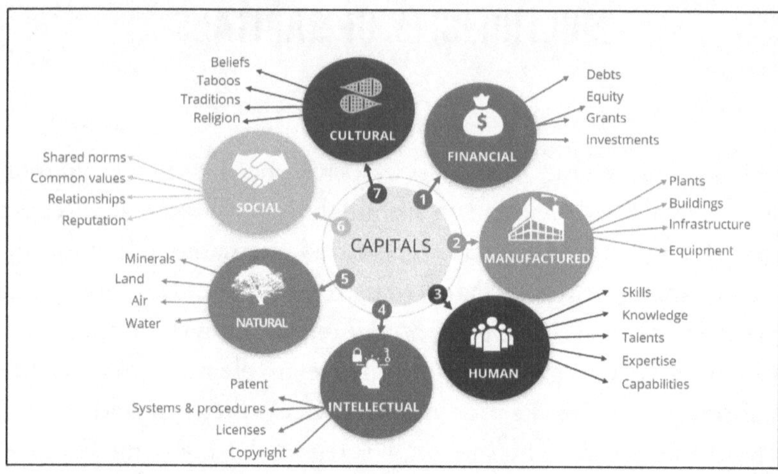

Figure 8 - The Seven Business Capitals Model

As complex and beyond-scope as the multiple capitals concept may seem to a typical African SME, it is worth considering if it can contribute to value creation and enhance success. SMEs who develop an understanding of the different types of capital are better positioned to increase their value and aid in their business strategy as their business evolves from stage to stage. This is because each of these capitals is a store of value that can be built up or run down over time, but which must be increased for a business (of any size) to be successful and profitable.

Describing the Capitals for SMEs

A description of the capitals provides a basis for understanding sustainability in terms of the economic concept of wealth creation for SMEs. An SME seeking to explore the concept of sustainability will maintain and, where possible, enhance these stocks of capitals rather than deplete or degrade them.

1. Financial Capital

Financial capital is the most familiar form of capital. This is the capital that covers assets in the form of cash or cash-like items such as shares and bonds. It is often said that cash is king. This expression is typically used in analyzing businesses or investment portfolios, indicating the importance of cash flow in the overall fiscal health of a business. If a business is not making money, even if the other capitals are being well managed, it cannot be sustainable. The financial capital is the pool of funds available to an organization for use in the production of goods or the provision of services.

An SME will not survive for long without financial capital—debt, equity, or, commonly, both. Whether it comes from family, friends, venture capitalists, crowdfunding, banks, the markets, or elsewhere, SMEs need money to create value. SMEs must decide what financing source to use as parts of their capital structure. SMEs need a clear understanding of how the business financial value is created, as well as the dependence on other forms of capital. To improve attainment to financial capital, SMEs need to get investment ready.

2. Manufactured Capital

Manufactured capital refers to material goods and infrastructure owned, leased, or controlled by the SME that contribute to production or service provision but do not become part of its output. The main components include buildings, infrastructure (transport networks, communications, waste disposal systems), and technologies (from simple tools and machines to IT and engineering). This capital is important because the efficient use of manufactured capital enables an SME to be agile and creative and increases the speed to market of its products and services.

Having raw materials, a well-trained and healthy workforce, and structures in place to communicate will be pointless without the manufactured capital required to turn raw materials into a saleable product. This capital should be flexible, innovative, and used to decrease resource usage and increase efficiency. This is important for SMEs who operate on very thin margins with little room for inefficient production.

3. Human Capital

This is the people dimension of a business, which is critical regardless of the size of the business. Human capital is composed of two aspects: quantity and quality. Quantity means the number of employees that an SME employs or has access to, while quality refers to the knowledge, skills, and abilities presented by the workforce.

Without a suitably educated and trained workforce, it is impossible for businesses to operate effectively and efficiently. Damaging the human capital by poor work standards has many detrimental impacts on the ability of any company to create value. Unfortunately, some SMEs do not realize the importance of good people-management practices. A business filled with individuals with the right knowledge, skills, and abilities, who are also committed and motivated, is much more likely to be a well-adjusted and highly functioning SME. Investment in human capital leads to an increase in performance of SMEs. For this reason, to improve human capital, there is a necessity for personal development by SME owners in the area of business and financial-management skills through training.

4. Intellectual Capital

This represents the intangible assets that provide a competitive advantage, and include the following:

- Intellectual property (e.g., trademarks, copyright, patents, software, designs, and brand equity)
- Organizational systems, processes, and protocols
- Goodwill and other intangibles, which the organization has developed, that are associated with the brand and the reputation

There is a debate about the importance and worth of intellectual capital. In the business world today, intellectual property is measured in tens of billions of dollars. Leveraging these assets via licensing agreements, brand extensions, line extensions, and joint ventures provides opportunities to increase organizational value.

Google's acquisition of Motorola Mobility in 2012, for example, seemed geared almost exclusively toward the value of Motorola's patent portfolio, and much of the value assigned by the market to companies is due to the patent portfolios embedded within the company. Additionally, the ideas and strategies developed via intellectual capital and intangible assets provide valuable insight into existing operations and future projects. SMEs should be astute regarding intellectual properties and exploring ways to secure their rights. Sometimes, it does not take a lot of effort to secure business's intellectual property, however, as the business matures this capital could be worth a lot money.

5. Natural Capital

This capital represents the resources that occur naturally on earth. Natural capital can be used by businesses to generate income and increase production. Many businesses use natural resources such as air, water, wind, solar, animals, and trees to operate their company and increase value over time. It should be noted that business activities can positively or negatively affect natural capital. This needs to be remembered and considered by SMEs, who tend to distance themselves from the environmental impact of businesses.

Companies may or may not own the natural assets they require to operate. Responsible businesses are expected to operate within the limits of enhancement or regeneration of the natural environment and not cause its depletion. Natural capital may seem like an asset class that pertains only to companies in the extractive industries such as oil/gas and mining, but it is relevant for all companies.

6. Social Capital

Social capital is often operationalized through the identification of networks and network relationships, sometimes defined by the strength of links, recurrent group activity such as the frequency of meetings and other formal interactions, as well as informal meeting and other social activities, and social and family relationships.[159] The adage "It is not what you know but who you know" is a key to success in life and business. While this adage is obviously a gross generalization, there is an element of truth in the axiom, which most SMEs can relate with. A significant measure of financial and personal success comes from developing thriving and mutually beneficial relationships that allow SMEs to attain their business goals.

Social capital has become a recent focus of interest in the effects of capital on entrepreneurship. Three types of social capital networks are typically discussed—the family network, the network formed by friends or other contacts, and the business networks and associations. Relationship with a range of stakeholders is useful for businesses to thrive, and these relationships, if well managed, provide a social license for the business to operate. Social and relationship capital includes shared norms, common values and behaviors, and key stakeholder relationships.

I came across a research paper that established how SMEs in Africa get around market failures and lack of formal institutions. African SMEs do this by creating private governance systems in the form of long-term business relationships and tight ethnically-based business networks. There are important links between these informal governance institutions and SME performance. As may be expected, such networks have been known to raise the performance of insiders and, in the sparse business environments of the Africa region, have attendant negative consequences for market participation of outsiders. This is often indicated through the determinants of access to supplier credit.[160]

Successful performance of SMEs sometimes depends on their social capital. Therefore, to improve social capital, SME owners and managers need to ensure that they maintain strong relations with customers, suppliers, commercial banks, government agencies and the community within which they operate. SME owners need to take responsibility to improve their relations, including attending seminars and trade fairs and joining trade associations.

7. Cultural Capital

As explained earlier, I encountered this dimension in a literature on family businesses. Cultural capital is reckoned to be the most intangible and delicate of the forms of capital. It primarily has to do with the mindsets, values, and ethos that the family carries forward from generation to generation. It could also relate to the cultural contexts within which the business operates. In Africa, there are cultural implication of some business decisions. Often SME owner/managers have to be aware of and attuned to the cultural nuances in making business decisions, establishing governance practices and recruitment choices. The cultural nuances that affect businesses go beyond the ability to greet or choose the correct gifts.

The influence of cultural factors on business is extensive. Culture affects how employees are managed and sometimes affects the functional areas of marketing, sales, and distribution. It can affect a company's analysis and decision on how best to enter a new market. Understanding and being sensitive to the local culture is a critical factor for any business to succeed.

Notable African values include large family practices, hard work, respect for senior members of the society, the extended family system, religion, value for private property, language, and many other facets. SMEs sometimes are more in touch with the cultural nuances due to their informal structures and practices. It is important, therefore, to ensure that paying attention to these cultural perspectives add value to the business. The evolution of cultural beliefs and practices over time can help to shape the success of the individuals in the business and that of the business.

Owing to the very nature of African SMEs, they are rooted in the territory of origin, sharing values and culture with the local communities and stakeholders. In Africa, the generally slow approach to decision-making does not mean local businesspeople are unable to make quick decisions. Rather, it reveals the cultural significance of consensus and consultation, which tends to guide the decision-making process in Africa's group-oriented cultures. In Southern Africa, the concept of *ubuntu* ("I am because we are") can be translated as "human kindness," but its meaning embodies the ideas of connection, community, and mutual caring for all. Businesses are expected to demonstrate *Ubuntu* in taking business decisions that could otherwise, potentially erode the connectivity and interdependency.

Determining Critical Capitals

It should be noted that these capitals do not have to be owned to be used by or for the business or to have a positive or negative influence on the organization. Factually, whether or not the capitals a business uses or affects are owned by that business, their availability, quality, and affordability can affect the long-term viability of the business model and, therefore, its ability to create value over time. This is particularly the case with respect to capitals that are in limited supply and are nonrenewable.

In addition, the International Integrated Reporting Framework clearly states that not all capitals are equally relevant or applicable to all companies at all times. While most businesses interact with all capitals to some extent, these interactions might be relatively minor or so indirect that they are not sufficiently important. It may, therefore, be inferred that the interaction of SMEs with these capitals may not be sufficiently significant to warrant disclosure or require a lot of effort to track.

It is important for value creation that a business knows how it makes money and what it needs to create money and value, both in the short term and the long term. This is especially important in SMEs. Owners and managers of small businesses need to take time out to ask the following questions:

- Where does the business want to go, and how does it intend to get there?
- How does the business make money?
- What capitals does the business need most to make money?
- How can the business sustain value creation in the short to medium term?
- What does the business need to sustain value creation in the long term?

- How does the business's governance structure (if one exists) support its ability to create value in the short, medium, and long term?

These are important questions for any business. When analyzing the answers to these questions, the SME owners/manager will be able to determine if they are putting their efforts into the wrong activities. This allows them to refocus and move their efforts and limited resources into that part of their business that will create value by deploying appropriate capitals.

It is important to consider future needs when identifying the resources, processes, and assets needed for business continuity, not just what is needed in the present. It is also important to remember and take into consideration the interconnectedness of the business's capitals. Think about the requirements for each of the seven types of capital mentioned above and establish which ones are important at the present stage of business evolution.

Deploying the Capitals

An often-cited limitation of SMEs is the unavailability of financial capital for business growth, development, and expansion. Having studied small businesses for many years, I have seen that a business does not survive solely by financial capital. There are other forms of capital that an astute small business can depend upon and deploy to great benefit. Large businesses are very conscious of these capitals and have a structured way of using them judiciously. Small businesses are less conscious and therefore are not focused on the possibilities that these forms of capital offer.

At different times in the life of a business, a variety of different forms of capital would need to be deployed for the success of the business. SME owners/managers have the responsibility for creating an appropriate oversight structure to support the ability of the business to create value by leveraging the seven capitals. The capitals that are important change over the life of the businesses; therefore, business owners/manager need to be careful in the deployment of capitals. Business owners/managers need to be aware of that which are important for the present but also that which will be important to their businesses in the future. They need to ensure that they can obtain, protect, and maintain those capitals.

According to the International Integrated Reporting Framework, value created by a business over time is expressed in increases, decreases, or transformations of the capitals triggered by the business activities. The framework also states that value has two interrelated aspects, the first being the value created for the business, enabling financial returns to the providers of financial capital, and the other being value created for other stakeholders. The value that a business creates for other stakeholders often affects its ability to create value for itself. For example, a business that can create value for its employees enjoys their loyalty and increased productivity, which reflects on the bottom line. Similarly, when a business creates value for the community, it secures its license to operate, which could reduce cost of engagement or dispute settlement.

The seven capitals model can be used to allow SMEs to develop a vision of what sustainability might look like for its own operations, products, and services. The vision is developed by considering what the business needs to do in order to maximize the value of each capital. However, a business needs to consider the impact of its activities on each of the capitals in an integrated way in order to avoid trade-offs that could be detrimental to the business. Using the model in this way for decision-making can lead to more sustainable outcomes.

Managing these capital assets in the long term is a dynamic and organic process through which SMEs can begin to achieve a balance between their environmental, social, and economic activities. The best way to achieve a sustainable future is through a systemic change.

According to the resource-based view of the firm, described in chapter 2, a business is examined for the complex, dynamic, and intangible resources and capabilities that are unique to it. These resources and capabilities—often referred to as organizational competencies are embedded in internal processes, decision-making body (board of directors), human resources, or other intangible assets—can provide the business with competitive advantages. SMEs that pay attention to these seven capitals can have potential advantages over SMEs that do not focus on these critical resources. The aim is then to ensure that all these capitals are well managed such that they improve over time, and that the appropriate mix is applied.

Defining the Cost of Capital

There is a cost to every capital; however, if efficiently utilized, the value inherent in that capital increases the worth of the business over time. In a financial context, there is an associated cost of acquiring capital to run a company. The cost of debt is based on the interest rate and yield to maturity of the debt. The cost of equity is an implied cost that is calculated using the capital asset pricing model (CAPM).

SMEs tend to pay close attention to the cost of financial capital. Less attention is paid to the cost of other forms of capitals, such as cultural capital, intellectual capital, and social capital. These capitals have associated costs that are not very visible or tangible and may go unnoticed in the short term.

Worthy of note is the fact that the stock of capitals is not fixed over time but evolves and can constantly flow between and within the capitals. An action to increase one capital my result in the diminution of another capital. For example, manufactured capital is increased when a business acquires new plants and equipment for production. This action reduces the financial capital. In effect, financial capital has been transformed into manufactured capital. Such increases, decreases, and transformations are happening constantly. Ordinarily, it is expected that the cumulative result of these flows will be increased value accruing to the business. This shows that the capitals are interrelated and constantly in a state of flow and transformation, although at different rates and with different net outcomes.

Sometimes there is also the issue of trade-off, whereby the increase of one capital can be at the detriment of another—for example, in a situation where the business owner/manager is happy to increase profit (maximization of financial capital) by not paying a fair wage to the employees or adopting other inappropriate human resource policies and practices (decreasing the value of human capital). This may appear beneficial in the short term but will have negative long-term repercussions when employee attrition rises or productivity drops. The SME owner/manager, therefore, needs to understand the dynamics of the capitals to ensure that the overall outcomes will be beneficial to the business in the long term.

Developing the Case for Capital Consideration

Why should SMEs consider this assortment of capitals being proffered by the International Integrated Reporting Council? How does an SME incorporate integrated thinking and integrated reporting in its business practices?

SME owners/managers in Africa need to be aware of the evolution of the discussion for integrated reporting. The B20 (the G20's business arm) recommended promoting integrated reporting as a key means of improving SME reporting.[161] And some commentators and researchers have written on integrated reporting's relevance and value to SMEs with a view to building trust around past and future performance.

Developing a better understanding of the capitals can help SMEs appreciate the core drivers of their business so they can implement a business model that will help them grow. Like large companies, SMEs leverage a range of capitals (resources and relationships) to create value. These capitals can release value over time while simultaneously growing their capacity as a store of value, if they are properly cultivated by SME owners/managers. Wealth maximization is the main objective of SMEs, and its capital structure shows how the business plans to resource its projects to meet this objective.

An SME with a good understanding of the factors that determine its ability to create value over time can make better decisions that result in better outcomes. This understanding includes the SME's use of and effect on all the capitals central to its business model and future strategies, thereby enhancing strategy planning, execution, and evaluation. An understanding of these capitals helps the SME owner/manager to assess the strengths of their business model, spot any deficiencies, and address them quickly. These understandings facilitate a forward-looking stance (refer to chapter 9) and sound strategic decision-making.

Today, society and stakeholders can make a claim on how much information they want from a business. Therefore, to be accorded a degree of credibility, businesses need to tell their story to various stakeholders, ranging from current and prospective equity investors, banks, and other providers of financial capital through to employees, customers, creditors, and other stakeholders. The balance sheet and profit-and-loss account, where they exist, do not often provide a complete picture as to the SME's ability to create value. These reports do not quite capture capitals such as employee expertise, customer loyalty, and intellectual property. While past financials are important, they are only one aspect of an SME's value creation story. The result is that many stakeholders of SMEs do not have enough information to make an informed decision. While, integrated reporting may appear better suited to larger SMEs, with formal structures and more demanding external stakeholders, smaller business can gain competitive advantage by being able to share their value stories.

Understandably, smaller business owners/managers are often too busy even to consider taking on any additional administrative task such as integrated reporting. However, insufficient thought today about tomorrow's strategy means SMEs may end up simply here today, gone tomorrow. Thinking through the core elements of the business can help ensure SMEs grow and prosper in a way that can have a positive impact economically, socially, and environmentally.

While SMEs are not mandated to produce integrated reports, adopting a model that helps them tell a succinct story externally and internally, providing the full picture, shows how the SME creates and will continue to create value. A publication titled *Creating Value for SMEs through Integrated Thinking: The Benefits of Integrated Reporting*,[162] was produced by the International Federation of Accountants (IFAC) and the International Integrated Reporting Council. This publication provides guidance for SMEs to help them not only to adopt integrated reporting but also realize its many benefits.

Chapter Summary: Points to Pause and Ponder

- "Capitals" are stocks of value that are inputs to a company's business model and are relied upon by the company for business success.
- The seven capitals are financial, manufactured, human, social, natural, intellectual, and cultural.
- All organizations depend on various forms of capital for their value creation and commercial viability.

- The capitals do not have to be owned to be used by or for the business or to have a positive or negative influence on the organization.
- SMEs should consider future needs when identifying the resources, processes, and assets needed for business continuity, not just what is needed in the present.
- The capitals that are important change over the life of the business; therefore, business owners/manager need to be judicious in the deployment of capitals.
- The seven capitals model helps SMEs to develop a vision of what sustainability might look like for their operations, products, and services.
- Managing these capitals in the long term is a dynamic and organic process through which SMEs can begin to achieve a balance between their environmental, social, and economic activities.
- An SME with a good understanding of the factors that determine its ability to create value over time can make better decisions that result in better outcomes.

CHAPTER 11

CONSIDERATION FOR GOVERNANCE OF FAMILY BUSINESSES

This chapter considers the governance of family-owned/run/managed businesses. This dimension was intentionally left to the end because of the uniqueness of family businesses and in order not to confuse the terms "family business" and "small business." There are many family businesses that are not small businesses. In fact, family businesses range from small- and medium-sized companies to large private and public conglomerates that operate in multiple industries and countries. Several books have been written on family businesses and the governance of such businesses. However, these books and most academic research showcase large companies as the focus. There are very few studies that specifically examine the influence of family ownership on the performance of small businesses and governance.

Prominent family businesses in Africa include the following:

- Kenyattas (family of Kenyan president Jomo Kenyatta, with interests in hotels, dairy, media, and banking)
- Dos Santoses (family of Angolan president Eduardo dos Santos, with interests in telecom, banking, and oil and gas)
- Motsepes (family of South African billionaire Patrice Tlhopane Motsepe, with vast interests in mining)
- Dangote (family of Nigerian billionaire Aliko Dangote, with interests in cement, industry, food, real estate, telecom, oil and gas, and banking)

- Sawiris (family of Egyptian billionaire Onsi Sawiris, with interests in construction, industry, and telecom)
- Ackermans (family of South African Raymond Ackerman, who pioneered the expansion of the large Pick N' Pay supermarket chain in Africa)

It is sometimes difficult to keep the two terms (small business and family business) separate because many small businesses are companies that are entirely owned by the members of one or more families. These companies are generally considered family businesses.[163] This chapter provides an understanding of the characteristics of family businesses, highlighting leading governance practices. I will also discuss the essential role that corporate governance plays in the success of any family business.

Family Business

According to Wikipedia, "a family business is a commercial organization in which decision-making is influenced by multiple generations of a family, related by blood or marriage or adoption, who has both the ability to influence the vision of the business and the willingness to use this ability to pursue unique goals. They are closely identified with the firm through leadership or ownership."[164]

Family businesses represent one of the foundations of the world business community. Their creation, growth, and longevity are critical to the success of the global economy. They are the most dominant form of business organization and represent over 85 percent of EU/US businesses. The importance of family business to the global economy is not in doubt.[165] Similarly, family businesses in Africa account for around an estimated 75 to 85 percent of the companies across Africa, family-owned companies remain the backbone to most African economies.[166]

A constant finding in the history of research on family-owned businesses is that family problems often overshadow corporate governance. A feature of family-owned enterprises is the lack of separation of ownership from control. Sometimes, the duties, responsibilities, and privileges of family members are not always clearly defined. Usually, in family-owned businesses, the family has the requisite voting power to dismiss boards or management unilaterally or to overrule their decisions. Thus, the concept of independent directors hardly prevails in these companies

The survival rate of most African family businesses beyond the founder's generation is extremely low. A *Forbes* article titled "The 10 Leading Family Businesses in Africa," contributed by Mfonobong Nsehe, buttresses the low survival rate of most African family businesses beyond the founder's generation, with the example of a late Nigerian business mogul. This well-known business mogul, at a point in time, was believed to be one of the wealthiest men in Africa. He successfully built one of Nigeria's biggest business empires, consisting of an airline, a chain of newspapers, extensive real estate, fisheries, and retail. After he died in 1998, his businesses began to crumble. None of them exist today.

Family Business Governance

Family business governance is a system of process and structures put in place at the highest level of the business, family, and ownership to make the best possible decisions regarding the direction of the company and assurance of accountability and control.[167] In family businesses, there are two disctinct realms in which governance is critical – the family and the business. Therefore, there are family governance and business governance structures in the overarching family business governance structure, and these are parallel.

Such parallel governance structures in the business can provide a useful framework for consultation between the business and the family. In a well-developed family business, this involves understanding how the business and its governance structure interact with the family and its structures. It is a system that assures the control, accountability, and direction of the company and the unity and commitment of its ownership.

Despite the advantages of family businesses over nonfamily businesses, family businesses can be uniquely tricky to govern. Some of the potential landmines include succession struggles, role conflicts, and rivalries among colleagues who are also family. The absence of a succession plan can have detrimental effects, particularly if the business has generally endured under paternalistic leadership. It has been noted that

> *family businesses are notoriously light in their use of bureaucracy. It is one of their appealing characteristics, and an aspect of their speed and flexibility in problem-solving. Their informality and intimacy make elaborate decision-making methods unnecessary. However, it is a common failing of all growing businesses that they do not recognize how growth is changing them. They are like a child who stays in short pants even when they're splitting at the seams.*[168]

Family Governance

Some family businesses find it useful to develop family governance structures (e.g., family assembly, family council) that are parallel to the business governance structures (i.e., shareholders' assembly, board) to address issues and interests of the family in relation to the business. The family governance structure helps to answer questions such as: "What processes are required for effective family decision making?" What decisions will the family oversee, and who will be allowed to participate?"

A family governance structure could take the form of a *family assembly*, which has all family members meeting annually to update each other on how the business is going, discuss certain issues, and get the opinions of those not formally involved in the governance of the business. Since all family members would be invited, it should be structured so that there are events for all age groups. Such an event can also be an opportunity for education, recreation, and emphasizing the family business culture.

In addition, there may be a *family council* that acts as an executive committee of the family assembly. This is comparable to a board in the corporate setting. It would be comprised of elected members representing different branches and age groups in the family and including both members who are employed in the business and those who are not. It would meet as often as necessary to address issues and interests in a semiformal manner. As a family grows into further generations, certain committees can be added to the family governance structure to address issues such as career planning, education, and development of family members.

One of the issues that a *family council* may want to address is taking the lead in drafting a family constitution or other governance documents, such as a family business protocol or simply a family mission statement. The family constitution is the most comprehensive type of family governance document and commonly covers the family's values and beliefs (mission statement) and family business principles or policies (on employment, ownership, business governance, family governance, conduct in the business and outside, the means of amending the constitution, e.g., majority voting). Such a document should be periodically revised to reflect the changing requirements of an evolving business and family. The process of drafting such a document is as important as its content. The family should feel involved in the process and have time to reflect on it and agree to it.

Business Governance

This book covers the gamut of what small business governance should be. Described in chapter 3 are the key elements of an effective governance framework that the business should adopt depending on its stage of business.

For many family businesses, a board of directors is the core component of business governance. However, for those businesses that do not have a board or has one that only exists on paper, there is still a need for a decision-making structure. Because it provides oversight, accountability, and, most importantly, helps to ensure continuity planning for an effective business transition across generations.

Succession planning is one of the major banes of family businesses. Good corporate governance practice requires the board to establish succession plans for key executives. This is both as a contingency for the unexpected departure of a key executive and to professionally develop and prepare future company leadership. This is important for family businesses where research has shown that about 70 percent of family businesses do not survive past the first generation and that "many intergenerational successions fail soon after the second generation takes control."[169]

The Corporate Governance Journey of Société de Transformation Alimentaire (STA SA)

Société de Transformation Alimentaire (STA SA), a family business, registered and operating in the Republic of Niger, is specialized in producing infant foods for children from six months to five years. Since 2001, it has been manufacturing and marketing complementary, supplementary, and treatment products for governments and NGOs associated with humanitarian work, especially ones affecting children's nutrition. Its ambition is to make products accessible to low-income households with the best quality standards.

In 2019, STA produced over 5600 metric tons of products, helping save over two million children from malnutrition in Niger and surrounding countries such as Chad, Nigeria, Mali, and a few more in the Sahara region. STA is the very first local production unit of ready to use therapeutic food "RUTF" and one of the largest food industries in Niger collaborating with MSF, Nutriset, UNICEF, WFP, ICRC, Save the Children, and more.

STA's corporate governance journey is fascinating. According to the CEO, Monsieur Ismael Barmou, defining an SME versus, a large company was challenging at first. One of his first experimentation of corporate governance, particularly in the Republic of Niger, was the definition of an SME.

> *"I thought our company as a small player compared to most of my competitors, yet again the company was considered as a big company as there are very few companies making as much turnover in the business landscape. Therefore, you are expected to contribute formally to what I call "development effort" by paying quite a number of dues to the government from various sources."*

Then, he had to cope with cultural business habits and corporate governance realities, which he was not used to, as he was coming from an Anglo-Saxon university and professional background. Finally, running a family business has its own challenges and burdens. One of his most challenging experiences in corporate governance is related to succession planning. Changing STA's management team from an older generation to the younger generation, and introducing new business strategies and visions.

> *"I also have to mention that I was going through all these challenges in my early 30's. Therefore, there were issues related to trust in new governance strategies for the company. All of these occurred in an environment where investors had little or no trust. And local authorities were not giving enough guarantees for fair legal business systems. My company ended up going through many issues, some of which ended up at court with shareholders disagreeing at times on matters as straightforward as positive growth strategies. Ultimately, we went from being a small company to one of the major players in Africa and even in the world in our line of business over a period of ten years."*

As a company grows, its corporate governance requirements and its capacity to adopt robust corporate governance practices change. In addition, the company's stakeholder expectations also change.

> *"Now, we have new challenges related to growing even bigger, and that also comes with quite a lot of difficulties we both have to face and go pass in terms of governance. These issues have to do with bringing new partners, sometimes new shareholders and investors, higher governance expectations from clients and partners. I guess that will be the challenge for the next ten years."*

Family business governance is really a means of formalizing the interaction between the business institution and the family institution to achieve the goals of both without jeopardizing the other. Research in another emerging market—Taiwan—concluded that the influence of family ownership on SME performance is "positive and significant"[170] and there is no reason not to achieve this for African SMEs.

The Effect of Family Ownership on SMEs

About 75 percent of new family-owned SMEs that are started eventually fail to become established businesses, and most family businesses in the SME sector have stagnated without growing. Research has estimated that only 14 percent of family businesses make it beyond the third generation. In South Africa, only one in four family businesses survive to the second generation, while only one in ten make it to the third generation. This is similar to the trend across Africa. The influence of family ownership on the performance of an SME is known to be both positive and negative; two sides of a coin. It would appear, from my experience and the review of the literature, that the positive aspects outweigh the negative aspects in the long term.

Traditional research of family businesses tends to focus on the negative relationship between the family and the business. The family is criticized for often treating the business as a family employment agency or a private bank by drawing scarce resources away from the business to satisfy family members' financial and nonfinancial needs. Or it limits top management positions to family members (regardless of their skills and expertise) instead of recruiting qualified and capable professional managers. Such a restricted labor pool potentially leads to competitive disadvantages and may adversely affect other employees' effort and productivity.

There is a school of thought, based on the agency theory, which emphasizes the possibility of wealth expropriation behaviors relating to the concentration of family ownership. There is also the issue of institutional overlap within family businesses. Institutional overlap refers to the coexistence of the family institution and the business institution, which sometimes have incompatible sets of values and norms. This influences the choice of corporate governance practices in family businesses.

Regardless of the bleak scenario above, family ownership of SMEs also has a positive effect. Based on the agency theory perspective, combining ownership and control can be advantageous because family owners can act to mitigate managerial entrenchment and expropriation. Therefore, in this case, the objectives of the owner and the business are aligned. Since the family's wealth is invested in the business capital, there are strong incentives to monitor the business's management and to maximize profitability.

From the resource-based perspective, having the family actively represented in the business has intangible benefits, such as enabling the business to develop long-term relations with stakeholders, such as customers, employees, suppliers, and bankers. Such relationships create trust and result in certain long-term economic benefits for family businesses. In addition, family owners focus on the business performance because it reflects family legacy and influences their family reputation and standing in the society. There is an interest in longer investment horizon as the family may want the business as an asset to pass on to succeeding generations. This reflects positively on the small family business performance. The potential advantages of family ownership are likely to be capitalized in small family businesses.

Although family ownership has both potential advantages and disadvantages, the ability of an SME to capitalize on these potential advantages largely depends on the quality of the interaction between business and family. Small-sized family businesses are expected to maintain the interface between business and family so that these potential advantages are likely to be capitalized. With effective corporate governance practices, SMEs are more likely to carry out strategic and succession planning and hence, on average, grow faster and live longer. Governance also assists in relationship management, sharpening management skills and creating a solid structure that is open to innovation.

The International Finance Corporation (IFC), developed and issued a *Family Business Governance Handbook*[171]. The handbook is a concise and practical description of essential family business governance components and suggests approaches to resolving common family business governance dilemmas, taking account of their peculiar characteristics. The issues it considers include:

... the roles often played by family members in a business

... the necessity of developing a clear family governance structure as different generations join the business

... the role, structure and composition of the board of directors (including the role of independent directors), and

... the impact of senior managers on the business and the importance of developing a CEO succession plan.

Kellogg's executive education program, Governing Family Enterprises, which I attended a few years ago, tackles family business governance topics and helps organizations maintain continuity as they grow. While these two resources cater mainly to larger family businesses, there are lessons to be gleaned by smaller businesses. There are also several other resources and programs that can be effectively leveraged.

Chapter Summary: Points to Pause and Ponder

- Family businesses constitute the world's oldest and most dominant form of business organization.
- A crucial feature of family-owned enterprises is the lack of separation of ownership from control, implying that directors and managers cannot be distinguished.
- The survival rate of most African family businesses beyond the founder's generation is extremely low.
- The most successful family businesses are those with the right balance between healthy family professional management and responsible business ownership.
- The advantages of family business include commitment, knowledge continuity, reliability, and pride in the company's image.
- Family business governance is a system of processes and structures put in place at the highest level of the business, family, and ownership to make the best possible decisions regarding the direction of the company and assurance of accountability and control.
- Family businesses need to adopt family governance structures with a certain degree of formalization if they are to function well. There is a need for them to make efforts to document the organizational structure, clearly spell out the roles and responsibilities of each family business member, and enforce accountability.
- Family businesses need to identify the potential successor and not assume that the eldest male will automatically take over the company.

CHAPTER 12

BRINGING IT TOGETHER – REFRAMING CG FOR SMES

As has been stated repeatedly in this book, SMEs are the bedrock of economic development in both developing and developed economies. But how can SMEs be positioned to thrive? Based on my interactions over the years with small business owners and managers, I have discovered that profitability, long-term growth, and survival are top priority.

Corporate governance is the system by which companies are directed and controlled to achieve profitability and long-term growth and survival of the enterprise. In Africa, as with most other emerging markets, corporate governance is still evolving, particularly regarding the SME sector. Even in African countries where corporate governance practices are more established, many companies do not recognize strategic value from good governance and are focused solely on compliance and box-ticking.

The changing SME lifecycle implies that companies may be termed small today and could evolve very quickly in a matter of years into a medium or large company. A sound corporate governance framework is very fungible and scalable; therefore, it can be applied to a wide range of businesses in terms of size, scope, and industry. It would be essential to bring the concepts and models described in this book together in a coherent piece, as each plays a role in promoting the appreciation and adoption of corporate governance principles for SMEs in Africa.

The Amalgamation

Various concepts and models introduced and discussed in this book are connected and interdependent. The amalgamation of these perspectives provides a holistic foundation for small businesses in Africa, to understand corporate governance and embrace its adoption.

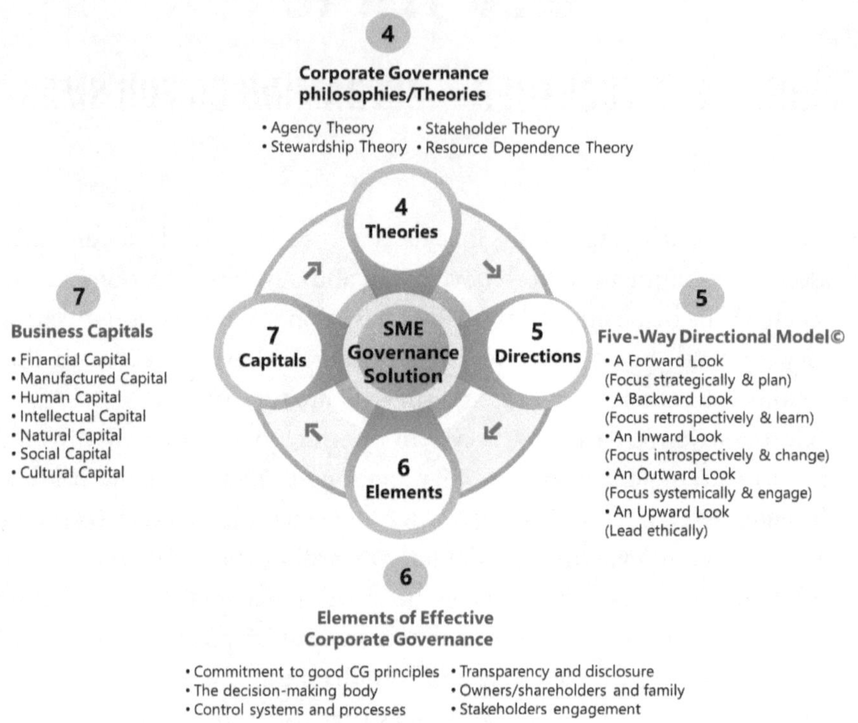

Figure 9 - Bringing it Together

There are four philosophies or theoretical perspectives of corporate governance that underpin the concept. There is merit in all theoretical perspectives, although they may not fully apply or apply at the same degree in the varying business forms of SMEs. Expectedly, there is no single (one-size-fits-all) corporate governance model, which will sufficiently provide for all types and forms of SMEs, as SMEs are usually at different stages in their business lifecycle. Therefore, to a significant extent, different corporate governance practices would apply to varying stages of business maturity.

Besides, a combination of features of different theoretical perspectives gives a robust understanding of the underlying issues. I believe that a multiplicity of theoretical perspectives provides the basis for understanding under which conditions each aspect is more applicable. Corporate governance systems are often (and should be) shaped by various factors, including business cultures, timelines, and business lifecycle.

My proprietary Five-Way Directional model© is one of the associated concepts of corporate governance that offers SMEs a simple way to view corporate governance practices, providing an opportunity for SME owners/managers to take another look at governance practices. In developing the model, consideration was given to the approaches that small business owners/managers should adopt with a description of how they contribute value to the business. Each of the five viewpoints connects with the corporate governance philosophies. This model will help business owners/managers to focus their attention in such a manner that they can ease the feeling of the frustration associated with (perceived) corporate governance ineptness.

Leveraging an existing model that outlines the key elements of sound corporate governance enhances the understanding of the concept. IFC's corporate governance methodology provides a consistent, distinct platform for understanding corporate governance. According to the IFC corporate governance methodology, there are six key elements that companies need to pay attention to, for a sound corporate governance framework. These elements are consistent with the corporate governance philosophies and the Five-Way Directional model©. In analyzing these elements, it was necessary to describe them from my knowledge of SMEs' needs and what can be adopted.

The seven business capitals were examined, in line with the International Integrated Reporting Framework. The capitals are *stocks of value* that companies rely upon for business success. These capitals can be increased, decreased, or transformed through a company's business activities to create value. A discussion about multiple capitals may seem farfetched to a typical African SME; however, SME owners/managers who develop an understanding of these business capitals will be better placed to support his/her business as it transitions from stage to stage.

The four philosophies, Five-Way Directional Model©, six elements of corporate governance, and the seven business capitals, are complementary. Steps for making corporate governance improvements require focusing on these multiple aspects of governance. The commitment of owners/managers of SMEs to sound governance practices is vital. Other matters to pay attention to include the strengthening of the role and responsibilities of the board of directors, improving the control environment, promoting disclosure and transparency, protecting shareholder rights, and engaging with stakeholders. An understanding of the attributes of each concept and model will enhance the capacity for adopting sound corporate governance practices.

A Quick Guide to Corporate Governance Practices for SMEs

Below is a summary of the potential corporate governance challenges, to help SME owners/managers to understand better the challenges they face or are likely to face in the varying stages of growth. The suggested practices are also aligned with the growth stages and offer guidance on how SME owners/managers can address the challenges from a corporate governance perspective.

The information provided will help SME owners/managers to take a practical approach to increasingly implementing better corporate governance policies, practices, and structures as the business transitions from stage to stage. The list of suggested practices is not comprehensive or prescriptive but provides general guidance. The practices should be tailored, taking into cognizance the legal and regulatory framework in the country of operation, ownership structure, size of the SME, and its business environment.

Stages	Potential corporate governance challenges	Corporate governance practices to consider
One: *Business Conception. Starting Up*	• Long-term investment goals but short-term financing capacity • Solo decision-making and overreliance on the founder, creating a key-person risk • Poor cash-flow management • Pricing products or services too high or too low • Mixing of family, personal and business interests, including money • Not preparing a realistic budget • Lack of formal processes and systems	• Consider an advisory board • Develop a formal business plan and draw up a strategy • Craft a simple organizational structure (this will usually evolve very quickly) • Determine whom to involve in decision-making or engage informal external advisers as required • Maintain basic bookkeeping records • Create a budget and use it • Develop the cash-flow records (capturing inflows and outflows) • Separate business bank accounts from that of the owner's • Establish the necessary regulatory requirements and seek compliance • Draft a shareholders' agreement/partnership agreement

Stages	Potential corporate governance challenges	Corporate governance practices to consider
Two: Active Growth. Ramping Up	• Solo or unilateral decision-making • Weak people management, siloed organization • Rudimentary and fragmented internal control systems • Inadequate cash-flow planning • Overwhelmed operations • Misalignment between supply and demand	• Create an outline of standard policies and processes • Develop a framework of crucial decisions required to manage the business • Decide on authority limits of key personnel • Establish accounting policies and reports needed internally and externally • Establish monthly bank account reconciliation reporting processes • Establish cash control mechanisms • Formalize shareholder agreements/partnership agreement • Prepare financial statements and audit per national accounting standards

Stages	Potential corporate governance challenges	Corporate governance practices to consider
Three: Organizational Development and Maintenance	• Operational inefficiencies as the business struggle to formalize its processes and policies • Decentralization and delegation can become unstable or unclear with new hires • New vs. Old staff dichotomy could create conflict • Poor corporate planning and execution • Inconsistent budget • Frequent power shifts or changes in key management positions • Lack of controls and accountability and an excessive focus on process	• Hire professionals for core operational and management positions. • Continue to refine the organization chart, key policies, and statements of fundamental business principles established. • Develop and document strategic plans and budgets. • Consider a functional/formal board (start small). • Establish a clear division of responsibilities and authorities between management and the board of directors. • Increase delegation (must be supported by improved internal controls). • Establish the internal audit function or as an outsource function. • Present necessary performance reports to external advisers or stakeholders.

Stages	Potential corporate governance challenges	Corporate governance practices to consider
Four: Business Expansion. Moving On and Up	• The management team could comprise of "stooges," with control still resting with founders and family members • Inability to keep employees motivated (and happy!) • Greater operational challenges • Less agility, leading to slow, bureaucratic processes. • The potential loss of momentum and creativity—the focus is more internal than on the market • Decreased sales due to failure to innovate	• Initiate documentation of core governance processes • Establish a formal board with appropriate committee structures. • Develop governance code, charters, and policies. • Develop formal HR policies to attract, retain, and motivate employees. • Initiate a succession-planning framework for critical persons. • Ensure the external auditor examines internal controls in the conduct of the audit. • Formally adopt written governance policies, such as code of ethics/code of conduct, whistleblowing CG code with E&S considerations; succession plan; HR/grievance mechanism).

Stages	Potential corporate governance challenges	Corporate governance practices to consider
Five: Sustainability. Staying on Track	• Lack of skills to consolidate and control the financial gains • The potential loss of entrepreneurial spirit • Potential inefficiencies due to rapid growth • Sibling rivalry • Succession problems • The potential tension between the entrepreneur and investors	• Separate roles of chairman and chief executive officer • An active board with an appropriate mix of independence, skills, and experience • A board induction and regular training, including training on relevant industry E&S issues • A board performance evaluation process and regular review of its composition • Enhanced risk-management processes: board approves risk, routinely monitors risk management and compliance with policies and procedures

It is worthy of note that although an effort was made to align the practices to the lifecycle stages, this does not necessarily mean exclusivity. This means that one practice can address several challenges and be relevant in multiple stages, e.g., having an advisory board, outsourcing specialist functions such as internal audit/controls etc.

Making the Corporate Governance Changes Stick

According to one of McKinsey's articles titled Changing change management, 70% of organizational change efforts fail or fall significantly short of fulfilling their change vision; sadly, most fail in the early stages. The main reason why these changes do not stick is a lack of leadership commitment to the change effort. How can SME owners/managers ensure that corporate governance changes are meaningful to the company and added expected value? In my years of supporting corporate governance changes, I have garnered the theories, methodologies, and organizational practices that business owners/managers need to establish lasting change. Below, I have combined learnings from my own experiences as a business leader and a corporate governance practitioner, with research and stories from others.

i. *Create a vision.* The first step should be for the leader (owner/manager) to commit to embracing corporate governance as a business culture. Commitment will signal to key stakeholders (such as employees and investors) the seriousness of the SME toward profitable and sustainable growth. There should be a recognition that good governance is not just about compliance (i.e., compliance with legislation, regulation, and codes of practice) but more about performance (i.e., improving the performance of the business through the formalization of structures, policies, and processes). The owner/manager should establish the purpose and expected benefits to guide the company. Many entrepreneurs are perceived as "ideas people." Sometimes these ideas do not seem realistic to others. It is essential to take time to explain what and why something new is being done; otherwise, the organizational infrastructure that is essential to survival can be left behind.

ii. *Establish the context and a plan.* Next, SME owner/manager should figure out what stage of growth the business is currently operating in (refer to chapter 5). The company needs to have developed to the point that decision-makers are starting to look for governance solutions that will help them to run the business more efficiently, effectively, and sustainably. Create an immediate action plan that includes a listing of the short-term high-priority changes identified. SMEs need to "grow into governance," by understanding the governance evolution (see chapter 5). This will help them to embark on the journey without being overwhelmed by the gamut changes required. Also, this context should be shared with others to gain their buy-in to the governance changes.

iii. *Identify strengths and weaknesses.* It is essential at this stage to engage in self-evaluation (refer to chapter 9: "Another Look at

Governance Practices"). An inward look with an introspective focus will help the SME owner/manager to determine what areas need improvement. It may be worthwhile to review existing internal structures and frameworks, establishing the strengths and weaknesses. This should also prepare the SME on a realistic timeline to implement the improvements. Regardless of the strengths or weaknesses of current company practices, corporate governance improvement is a matter of constant process. It takes time for all measures to be implemented. It also takes time for them to become rooted in the company as part of the corporate culture. Understanding your business and its specific needs for governance change helps to make the change stick.

iv. *Define responsibilities.* Thinking through how best to govern the governance improvements will ensure the effectiveness of implementation efforts. There are various alternatives, such as expanding the scope of responsibility for an existing body or a company official who is tasked with this function or seek external support. Companies at this level have limited resources—of both "spare" finances and management's time—so it is critical to select a realistic approach. Regardless of the approach, it is vital to involve the company's senior leaders—the board, senior management, and perhaps controlling shareholders. Assign clear responsibilities for monitoring governance-related actions to ensure that company leaders receive relevant and timely information on progress and have sufficient opportunity to intervene and make course corrections if needed.

v. *Monitor the evolving governance.* Having the right set of policies, practices, and structures is not enough to ensure that changes in governance will really take place. It is essential to keep an eye on how the implementation efforts are going. Monitoring is key to making things work properly. The governance system must be monitored along the way so that it can be adapted to new (internal and external) situations and to ensure that knowledge and information related to earlier governance efforts are captured. Special attention has to be given to creating and maintaining an efficient decision-making process and ensuring good information flow. This includes the new practices and the mechanisms to facilitate their implementation and continuous improvement.

Some corporate governance practices will be unique to your company, depending on several factors. These factors include the legal and regulatory framework in the country of operation, ownership structure, size of the SME, motivation for improvements, stage of the company's development, and prevalent corporate culture and traditions. Despite the uniqueness of individual company governance needs, good governance practices are based on internationally and domestically recognized principles and standards of best practices. Therefore, adapt your company's corporate governance initiative to the regional and country context.

Chapter Summary: Points to Pause and Ponder

- Profitability, long-term growth, and survival are of paramount interest to SMEs in Africa and should be to the government too since SMEs are the bedrock of economic development.
- SME lifecycle implies that companies may be termed small today and could evolve very quickly in a matter of years into a medium or large company.
- A sound corporate governance framework is scalable and can be applied to a wide range of businesses in terms of size, scope, and industry.
- The concepts and models introduced and discussed in this book are connected and interdependent. The amalgamation of these perspectives provides a holistic foundation for small businesses in Africa, to understand corporate governance and embrace its adoption
- The four philosophies, five directions, six elements of corporate governance, and the seven business capitals, are complementary.
- About 70 percent of organizational change efforts fail or fall significantly short of fulfilling their change vision, mainly due to a lack of leadership commitment to the change effort.
- To make corporate governance changes stick -

o   *create the vision*
o   *establish the context and a plan*
o   *identify strengths and weaknesses*
o   *define responsibilities*
o   *monitor the evolving governance*

CONCLUSION

Issues of corporate governance remain relevant to emerging countries and small businesses operating in these countries. Some say that the widespread existence of small (family and non-family) businesses that do not have their shares listed may be a reason for the low insistence on good corporate governance in these economies. However, the view that issues of corporate governance are less relevant to small businesses in emerging economies is flawed. Good public governance allows citizens to ascertain whether their interests are being served effectively. Similarly, corporate organizations, irrespective of their size, must strive to strengthen their governance practices so that their shareholders and stakeholders can make reasonable investment and engagement decisions.

SMEs need to view corporate governance from the lens of the benefits to the business. Good corporate governance practices contribute significant value, a strong ethical culture, good performance, effective control, and a license to operate. These are advantageous to businesses of any size, and an SME that adopts good corporate governance gains competitive advantages.

However, applicability remains very important, and regulators across Africa are beginning to consider corporate governance in a way that is appropriate for SMEs. The ability to compete and succeed over decades—and even longer—is every entrepreneur's dream. Business longevity hinges upon nuanced growth strategies and requires strategic engagement with the business stakeholders. Corporate governance does help.

Currently, most emergent economies are faced with the concern of how to establish the groundwork for long-term economic performance and competitiveness. But this cannot be materialized without the existence of good corporate governance. Governments, directors, corporate owners, corporate managers, and other stakeholders in emerging markets have realized that good corporate governance practices are critical for a vibrant ecosystem and successful businesses.

The issues discussed in this book address the importance of corporate governance for small businesses in Africa, taking into cognizance the challenges that some of these small businesses face in adopting corporate governance. The discussion was approached practically, describing how corporate governance can support the quest of every small business owner/manager for a successful enterprise.

In a Nutshell: A Quick Recap

This book is a chronicle of sorts, with an evergreen collection of nuggets for action learning. It presents an invitation to all SMEs in Africa to learn and act, and act and learn. This is a cycle for effective and sustainable progression.

The opening chapter presents the concept of corporate governance as the system by which companies are directed and controlled. This system produces specific positive outcomes for businesses. Focusing on these outcomes should propel an SME to seek and adopt good corporate governance practices.

Chapter 2 goes into the archives and digs up the enduring corporate governance philosophies—agency theory, stewardship theory, stakeholder theory, and resource dependence theory. The analysis of these philosophies provides a connection between the original theories and current corporate governance practices and shows how these are relevant to SMEs. These theories are the foundation for building strong governance frameworks.

The third chapter presents the six key elements (building blocks) for a sound corporate governance framework. These are, commitment to good corporate governance principles, the decision-making body, control system and processes, transparency and disclosure, matters relating to the owners/shareholders, and stakeholder engagement. An effort was made to consider these elements and connected them to the realities of an SME in Africa.

The fourth chapter dives into the world of SMEs, analyzing the great importance of SMEs as the heartbeat of job creation and the engine of economic development in Africa. SMEs represent a nation's entrepreneurship talent and potential for innovation, which enables an economy to thrive. Therefore, governments must nurture SMEs and encourage their innate ability to create value.

Chapter 5 discusses the stages of business growth and development for SMEs. The key message being that SMEs will necessarily evolve and go through different stages of growth, characterized by differing organizational structures, and varied management styles. There are five typical stages of growth that every business will experience, each with its own set of challenges. In these different stages, different corporate governance practices would be appropriate. Therefore, there should be no pressure on SMEs to advance beyond the level relevant to its stage of growth. Otherwise, there will be a strain on the capacity of the business or corporate governance practices will become superficial.

The sixth chapter explores the dichotomy of SMEs and corporate governance, capturing the various reasons that SMEs fail. Sound corporate governance structures and practices can make a positive difference. SME owners/managers need to learn from the mistakes and missteps of their progenitors. It was necessary to delve into the debatable application of corporate governance for SMEs, concluding that corporate governance is not a one-size-fits-all concept. This chapter also highlights what small businesses need, capturing what keeps a typical SME owner/manager awake at night. SMEs are concerned about attracting finance, achieving profitability and growth, and passing on a viable business to the next generation. These concerns make it clear that corporate governance for SMEs is not an oxymoron.

Chapter 7 unveils the outcome of a personal action learning research, which polled the views of SMEs on the gains and pains of adopting good corporate governance practices. It also explores the Catch-22 scenario, whereby the areas that add the most value are the same areas that SMEs struggle the most with.

Chapter 8 considers the views of other stakeholders. For SMEs, high-quality relationships with financiers, customers, suppliers, employees, and the local community underpin their value. It was, therefore, essential to provide an understanding of their perspectives and suggesting some implications of corporate governance for SME. There are also suggestions on how these stakeholders can help SMEs improve the adoption of good corporate governance practices.

The ninth chapter presents a unique look at corporate governance from different directions to help SMEs visualize the business implications of their actions (or inactions). SMEs are shown how to look at corporate governance through the lens of the Five-Way Directional model©. This is designed to help SMEs focus their attention in such a manner that they can ease the feeling of the frustration associated with corporate governance ineptness. This requires them to look forward strategically, look backward retrospectively, and look inward look introspectively. They must also look outward systemically and look upward, acknowledging their accountabilities and make ethical decisions.

Chapter 10 delves into the sustainability arena, based on the framework of the International Integrated Reporting Council, also cited in the *King IV Report*. The discussion centers on the types of business capitals, which are stocks of value. These capitals, which are inputs to a company's business model, are relied upon by the company for business success. The capitals are financial capital, manufactured capital, human capital, social and relationship capital, natural capital, intellectual capital, and cultural capital. Understanding and exploring the dynamics of these capitals help SMEs to improve business practices, engage better with stakeholders, and ensure business growth with a positive impact economically, socially, and environmentally.

The eleventh chapter provides consideration for the governance of family businesses. Family businesses range from small- and medium-sized companies to large private and public conglomerates that operate in multiple industries and countries. Therefore, while most SMEs are family-owned/managed businesses, most family businesses are not SMEs. While delineating the family institution from the business institution, this chapter also provides a view on the effect of family ownership on SMEs.

What Next?

A book such as this should typically end with the next steps, *right*?

This is the point in time when all the great ideas and models on corporate governance for SMEs in the book get funneled into clear, definable, and achievable...next steps. Now, the rubber meets the road!

The introduction of new corporate governance practices or

improvement of existing practices necessarily causes significant changes to a business, which makes it a change-management process. One of the main challenges for SMEs to make corporate governance changes is a mindset change for the owners/leaders. It is more cost-effective and efficient to start implementing corporate governance at the very early stages of the business. However, it is never too late to start, and the exact solutions and tools will evolve and come together with the business as it grows.

Business owners/leaders are responsible for the implementation of corporate changes. Success in improving corporate governance policies and practices requires the company's leadership to take responsibility for ensuring that governance changes are implemented. Such oversight and support for implementation set the proper tone at the top, which, when combined with adequate mechanisms for monitoring and following up, can help to ensure successful implementation. It also helps the company to become ready to start adopting (and benefiting from) not only individual good corporate governance policies and practices but also the corporate governance system as a whole.

Good governance is not a badge of honor. It requires continuous improvement to stay relevant. All interested parties must realize that good governance requires constant improvement as internal and external circumstances change. SMEs should implement the best practices possible for the benefit of the business, its owners, and all stakeholders.

SMEs are all different in their needs and purpose. Corporate governance, therefore, needs to be applied differently to deal with the various issues within a business in a way that suits that business. SMEs owners/managers need to understand that there is a process to change, and this should be followed for change to be successful.

Corporate governance is only possible if you truly believe in it. It is tough to precisely measure its results, especially in the short term. But every time that you look back, you know that a long way has been walked, and it becomes harder and harder to step back.
—João Elek, NET, CFO

Final Reflections

- Definitions of an SME vary from region to region, and presumably, in a few years, this may evolve further. However, regardless of the notion of the evolving definition of SMEs, the outcome of the content of this book remains relevant and useable as companies will transition through various stages of business growth and, therefore, will engage with the concept of corporate governance as appropriate for the stage of business development.

- At what point can a company outgrow its corporate governance framework? Issues of corporate governance are very fungible and scalable and, therefore, can be applied to a wide range of businesses. Another way SMEs differ from their larger counterparts is their highly dynamic nature. Challenges faced by SMEs change dramatically as they grow and as they experience changes in their organizational, management, and ownership structures.

- From years of working as a corporate governance professional in Africa, I have discovered that companies and individuals (who run these companies) do not have a common understanding of corporate governance and its various benefits (and, of course, challenges). There is a dire need to educate and create an appropriate level of awareness to gain access to and assist the SME to adopt corporate governance standards and practices. It is also vital to create opportunities to educate and enlighten SMEs on the business case for corporate governance in the West African context.

- There is always the perception in some markets that if corporate governance is such a great idea, then companies in developed economies ought not to fail as they are the proponents of good corporate governance standards and practices. This brings to question the form versus substance of corporate governance adoption. The box-ticking exercise versus real commitment to implement corporate governance. There should be a way to separate the form (i.e., box-ticking) from the substance (i.e., real commitment).

- Businesses are getting more creative as the business environment gets more complicated. How does this affect corporate governance (if at all)? In this era of artificial intelligence and robotics, do corporate governance structures, principles, and frameworks apply? A new way of thinking about the convergence of corporate governance and technological innovation is required. However, every business model requires decision-making and operational implementation of strategic intent and decisions, and corporate governance enables both.

A friend once shared this profound insight, and I couldn't have said it better:

*"From a governance point of view, you simply have to do what
is right, right from the start, rather than wait until much later.
Sometimes, for startups, they tend to think that getting the governance
structure right is expensive, that it takes too much time, but I think
that it's worth their while to make sure they get it right."*

Big journeys begin with small steps. I hope every small business owner/ manager will take the required small steps to start early and keep improving their corporate governance practices.

A goal without a plan is a wish. I hope every small business owner/ manager will make the required commitment and make definite plans toward the adoption of corporate governance and reap the many benefits

POSTFACE

As stated at the onset, this book is the foundation for my vision to develop and facilitate growth programs for African SMEs. As I continue in my mission to help SMEs improve their corporate governance systems, certain things have become more apparent.

First is the notion that a sound corporate governance system is not a nicety or luxury; it is the key to business survival. Even more critical is the fact that governance is not *just* a key to business survival; it is actually a crucial source of competitive advantage and leverage for continuity. Also, small business owners/managers cannot afford to ignore it or pretend that it does not relate to them.

The second insight from my reflections might be even more important. Adopting corporate governance is not something you do once and then forget about it. It is not a quick-fix or short-term solution to a nagging business problem. Corporate governance adoption is a long-term commitment` to a new way of working that takes time to mature, build momentum, and demonstrate clear value. Corporate governance is not a destination but a journey; it is not a sprint but a marathon.

The third insight is that no small business owner/manager can implement corporate governance improvements on their own. It must be a team effort, but the owner/manager must take a strategic lead. Setting the tone at the top is a critical success factor. Governance as a tool for performance improvement, and it is only as effective as its implementation is successful.

The ideas, experiences, and perspectives I have offered in this book provide sufficient guidance, relevant tools and a road map for the effort required. I fully intend to continue to observe, record, and interpret this field of study and practice because of the enormous contribution that corporate governance can make in the economic landscape across Africa. This is my way of informing you that I am committed to this journey and intend to turn this book into a living, growing knowledge base – supplemented by my blog (https://smecgcoach.wixsite.com/coach), to create ongoing support to, and conversation with an engaged community of SMEs in Africa and beyond.

A conversation is a two-way exchange of ideas and information, and a community is a multidimensional version of a conversation spread out over a period of time and space. I encourage you to join me as I look forward and move ahead.

ABOUT THE AUTHOR

Dr. Chinyere Almona heads the Africa Corporate Governance (Advisory) Program at the International Finance Corporation (part of the World Bank Group), which provides a variety of corporate governance (CG) interventions across Sub-Saharan Africa; covering: Nigeria, Ghana, Sierra Leone, Liberia, Cote D'Ivoire, Senegal, Kenya, Uganda, Rwanda, Tanzania, Ethiopia & South Africa. A governance professional, with a strong vision and enthusiasm in helping clients adopt good CG practices.

Before joining the World Bank Group, Dr. Almona was a Director at PricewaterhouseCoopers' Advisory Consulting Practice in Nigeria, heading the firm's Governance, Risk and Compliance Practice, which she established. International management consulting professional with a specialist MBA in Corporate Social Responsibility from the University of Nottingham, UK. She is a Fellow of the Institute of Chartered Accountant of Nigeria, an Honorary Fellow of the Institute of Directors (Ghana), holds a Doctorate Degree in Business Administration, and about three decades of work experience.

Dr. Almona has led various CG reforms in the African region, such as development and revision of CG regulations working with Central Banks, Stock Exchanges and Capital Market Authorities, establishing governance courses in major universities, and developing governance frameworks for SMEs. She is passionate about the role of governance in supporting SMEs to grow and contribute significantly to their respective country's economy.

She has contributed extensively to research on corporate governance, leadership, corporate responsibility, and women on boards. She has a robust Pan-African perspective as an alumna of the British Council's

Pan-African InterAction Leadership Program, aimed at building leaders with a heart for Africa. She is a published author of four other books, an international speaker, a board advisor, an IFC certified trainer, and a certified leadership coach

@chinyerealmona   www.linkedin.com/in/chinyerealmona/

ENDNOTES

1   Okeahalam, Charles C., and Oludele A. Akinboade. "A review of corporate governance in Africa: Literature, issues and challenges." In *global corporate governance forum*, vol. 15, no. 1, pp. 1-34. 2003.

2   Mervyn King, King Report on Corporate Governance for South Africa (King II Report) (Parktown, South Africa: Institute of Directors in Southern Africa, 2002), p.18.

3   King IV Report on Corporate Governance for South Africa, 2016

4   World Bank publication 'Corporate Governance: A Framework for Implementation' (September 1999)

5   Rwegasira, K. (2000). Corporate Governance in Emerging Capital Markets: whither Africa? Corporate Governance: An International Review, 8(3), 258

6   Goergen, M., Brewster, C., & Wood, G. (2010). Corporate Governance: Nonequity Stakeholders. *Corporate Governance: A Synthesis of Theory, Research, and Practice*, 469-495.

7   Mark, R. (2011), "The quality of corporate governance within financial firms in stressed markets," in Hawley, J.P., Kamath, S.J. and Williams, A.T. (Eds), Corporate Governance Failures: The Role of Institutional Investors in the Global Financial Crisis, University of Pennsylvania Press, Philadelphia, PA.

8   Fisher, Richard, and Harvey Rosenblum (2013), Vanquishing Too Big to Fail, 2012 Annual Report (Dallas: Federal Reserve Bank of Dallas), www.dallasfed. org/microsites/fed/annual/2012/ar12b/index.pdf

9   Letza, S., Sun, X., & Kirkbride, J. (2004). Shareholding versus stakeholding: A critical review of corporate governance. *Corporate Governance: An International Review, 12*(3), 242-262

10 Abeysekera, I. (2013). A template for integrated reporting. Journal of Intellectual Capital, 14(2), 227-245

11 Krechovská, Michaela, and Petra Taušl Procházková. "Sustainability and its integration into corporate governance focusing on corporate performance management and reporting." *Procedia Engineering* 69 (2014): 1144-1151.

12 Deegan, C. (2002). Introduction: The legitimising effect of social and environmental disclosures–a theoretical foundation. Accounting, Auditing & Accountability Journal, 15(3), 282-311

13 Abor, J., & Biekpe, N. (2007). Corporate governance, ownership structure and performance of SMEs in Ghana: implications for financing opportunities. *Corporate Governance: The international journal of business in society*, *7*(3), 288-300

14 Bebchuk and Cohen, 2004; Bebchuk, Cohen and Ferrell, 2004; Kyereboah-Coleman and Biepke, 2006a; Kyereboah-Coleman and Biekpe, 2006b; Kyereboah-Coleman and Biekpe 2006c

15 Ibid.

16 Johnson, S., Boone, P., Breach, A. and Friedman, E. (2000), "Corporate governance in the Asian financial crisis", Journal of Financial Economics, 58(1–2), pp. 141-186

17 Atkinson, T., Luttrell, D. and Rosenblum, H., 2013. How bad was it? The costs and consequences of the 2007–09 financial crisis. Staff Papers, (Jul).

18 Reinhart, C.M. and Rogoff, K.S., 2008. Is the 2007 US sub-prime financial crisis so different? An international historical comparison (No. w13761). National Bureau of Economic Research.

19 Berglöf, E., & Claessens, S. (2006). Enforcement and good corporate governance in developing countries and transition economies. *The World Bank Research Observer*, *21*(1), 123-150

20 Nicholson, G. J., & Kiel, G. C. (2007). Can directors impact performance? A case-based test of three theories of corporate governance. *Corporate Governance: An International Review*, *15*(4), 585-608; OECD, 1998 cited by Mulili, Benjamin Mwanzia, and Peter Wong. "Corporate governance practices in developing countries: The case for Kenya." *International journal of business administration* 2, no. 1 (2011): 14.

21 Claessens, Stijn, and B. Burcin Yurtoglu. "Corporate governance in emerging markets: A survey." *Emerging markets review* 15 (2013): 1-33.

22 https://en.wikipedia.org/wiki/Medici_Bank#cite_note-1

23 Salvato, Carlo, and Guido Corbetta. "Transitional leadership of advisors as a facilitator of successors' leadership construction." *Family business review* 26, no. 3 (2013): 235-255; Madison, K., Holt, D. T., Kellermanns, F. W., & Ranft, A. L. (2016). Viewing family firm behavior and governance through the lens of agency and stewardship theories. *Family Business Review*, *29*(1), 65-93.

24 Abdullah, Haslinda, and Benedict Valentine. "Fundamental and ethics theories of corporate governance." *Middle Eastern Finance and Economics* 4, no. 4 (2009): 88-96.

25 Hillman, A. J., Withers, M. C., & Collins, B. J. (2009). Resource dependence theory: A review. *Journal of management*, *35*(6), 1404-1427. Hill, C. W., &

Jones, T. M. (1992). Stakeholder-agency theory. *Journal of management studies*, *29*(2), 131-154

26   Corbetta, G., & Salvato, C. A. (2004). The board of directors in family firms: one size fits all?. *Family Business Review*, *17*(2), 119-134. Hillman, A. J., & Dalziel, T. (2003). Boards of directors and firm performance: Integrating agency and resource dependence perspectives. *Academy of Management review*, *28*(3), 383-396

27   Corbetta, G., & Salvato, C. A. (2004). The board of directors in family firms: one size fits all?. *Family Business Review*, *17*(2), 119-134. Hillman, A. J., & Dalziel, T. (2003). Boards of directors and firm performance: Integrating agency and resource dependence perspectives. *Academy of Management review*, *28*(3), 383-396.

28   Pugliese, A., Minichilli, A., & Zattoni, A. (2014). Integrating agency and resource dependence theory: Firm profitability, industry regulation, and board task performance. Journal of Business Research, 67(6), 1189-1200

29   Hillman, A. J., & Dalziel, T. (2003). Boards of directors and firm performance: Integrating agency and resource dependence perspectives. *Academy of Management review*, *28*(3), 383-396

30   Madison, K., Holt, D. T., Kellermanns, F. W., & Ranft, A. L. (2016). Viewing family firm behavior and governance through the lens of agency and stewardship theories. *Family Business Review*, *29*(1), 65-93

31   Chrisman et al., 2004, cited by Madison, K., Holt, D. T., Kellermanns, F. W., & Ranft, A. L. (2016). Viewing family firm behavior and governance through the lens of agency and stewardship theories. *Family Business Review*, *29*(1), 65-93

32   Corbetta, G., & Salvato, C. A. (2004). The board of directors in family firms: one size fits all?. *Family Business Review*, *17*(2), 119-134. Hillman, A. J., & Dalziel, T. (2003). Boards of directors and firm performance: Integrating agency and resource dependence perspectives. *Academy of Management review*, *28*(3), 383-396

33   Gnan, L., Montemerlo, D., & Huse, M. (2015). Governance systems in family SMEs: The substitution effects between family councils and corporate governance mechanisms. *Journal of Small Business Management*, *53*(2), 355-381

34   Aronoff and Ward 1992; Salvato 2002 cited by Gnan, L., Montemerlo, D., & Huse, M. (2015). Governance systems in family SMEs: The substitution effects between family councils and corporate governance mechanisms. *Journal of Small Business Management*, *53*(2), 355-381)

35   Davis et al., 2010, cited by Madison, K., Holt, D. T., Kellermanns, F. W., & Ranft, A. L. (2016). Viewing family firm behavior and governance through the lens of agency and stewardship theories. *Family Business Review*, *29*(1), 65-93).

36   Tirole, 2001, cited by Ayuso, S., Rodríguez, M. A., García-Castro, R., & Ariño, M. A. (2014). Maximizing stakeholders' interests: An empirical analysis of the

stakeholder approach to corporate governance. *Business & society*, *53*(3), 414-439; Mason, C., & Simmons, J. (2014). Embedding corporate social responsibility in corporate governance: A stakeholder systems approach. *Journal of Business Ethics*, *119*(1), 77-86.

37 Ayuso, S., Rodríguez, M. A., García-Castro, R., & Ariño, M. A. (2014). Maximizing stakeholders' interests: An empirical analysis of the stakeholder approach to corporate governance. *Business & society*, *53*(3), 414-439; Pigé, B. (2017). Stakeholder theory and corporate governance: the nature of the board information. *Management: journal of contemporary management issues*, *7*(1), 1-17; Mason, C., & Simmons, J. (2014). Embedding corporate social responsibility in corporate governance: A stakeholder systems approach. *Journal of Business Ethics*, *119*(1), 77-86

38 Sachs & Riihli, 2011, cited by Harrison, J. S., & Wicks, A. C. (2013). Stakeholder theory, value, and firm performance. *Business ethics quarterly*, *23*(1), 97-124; Ayuso, S., Rodríguez, M. A., García-Castro, R., & Ariño, M. A. (2014). Maximizing stakeholders' interests: An empirical analysis of the stakeholder approach to corporate governance. *Business & society*, *53*(3), 414-439

39 Hillman, A. J., Withers, M. C., & Collins, B. J. (2009). Resource dependence theory: A review. *Journal of management*, *35*(6), 1404-1427.

40 Corbetta, G., & Salvato, C. A. (2004). The board of directors in family firms: one size fits all?. *Family Business Review*, *17*(2), 119-134. Hillman, A. J., & Dalziel, T. (2003). Boards of directors and firm performance: Integrating agency and resource dependence perspectives. *Academy of Management review*, *28*(3), 383-396

41 Pfeffer & Salancik, 1978 cited by Corbetta, G., & Salvato, C. A. (2004). The board of directors in family firms: one size fits all?. *Family Business Review*, *17*(2), 119-134. Hillman, A. J., & Dalziel, T. (2003). Boards of directors and firm performance: Integrating agency and resource dependence perspectives. *Academy of Management review*, *28*(3), 383-396

42 Corbetta, G., & Salvato, C. A. (2004). The board of directors in family firms: one size fits all?. *Family Business Review*, *17*(2), 119-134; Johannisson, Bengt, and Morten Huse. "Recruiting outside board members in the small family business: An ideological challenge." *Entrepreneurship & Regional Development* 12, no. 4 (2000): 353-378.

43 Hill, C. W., & Jones, T. M. (1992). Stakeholder-agency theory. *Journal of management studies*, *29*(2), 131-154; Gómez-Mejía, Luis R., Katalin Takács Haynes, Manuel Núñez-Nickel, Kathyrn JL Jacobson, and José Moyano-Fuentes. "Socioemotional wealth and business risks in family-controlled firms: Evidence from Spanish olive oil mills." *Administrative science quarterly* 52, no. 1 (2007): 106-137.

44 Cremers, K. J. (2015). Commitment and entrenchment in corporate governance. *Nw. UL Rev., 110,* 727.

45 O'Regan, Nicholas, Abby Ghobadian, and David Gallear. "In search of the drivers of high growth in manufacturing SMEs." *Technovation* 26, no. 1 (2006): 30-41..

46 Hambrick, D. C., Misangyi, V. F., & Park, C. A. (2015). The quad model for identifying a corporate director's potential for effective monitoring: Toward a new theory of board sufficiency. *Academy of Management Review, 40*(3), 323-344

47 Pletzer, J. L., Nikolova, R., Kedzior, K. K., & Voelpel, S. C. (2015). Does gender matter? Female representation on corporate boards and firm financial performance-A meta-analysis. *PloS one, 10*(6), e0130005

48 Liang and Li, 1999 cited by Mahzan, N., & Yan, C. M. (2014). Harnessing the benefits of corporate governance and internal audit: advice to SME. *Procedia-Social and Behavioral Sciences, 115,* 156-165

49 Melyoki, L. L. (2005). *Determinants of effective corporate governance in Tanzania.* University of Twente [Host]. Adeoye, A. A. (2015). The Impact of External Factors on Corporate Governance system of firms: Empirical Evidence from Sub-Saharan Africa Anglophone Countries (SSAA). Global Advanced Research Journal of Management and Business Studies, 4(1), 16-35; Azeez, A. A. (2015). Corporate governance and firm performance: evidence from Sri Lanka. *Journal of Finance, 3*(1), 180-189

50 Corbetta, G., & Salvato, C. A. (2004). The board of directors in family firms: one size fits all?. *Family Business Review, 17*(2), 119-134.

51 Carpenter, M. A., & Fredrickson, J. W. (2001). Top management teams, global strategic posture, and the moderating role of uncertainty. Academy of Management journal, 44(3), 533-545.

52 Siwangaza, L., Smit, Y., Juan-Pierré, B., & Ukpere, W. I. (2014). The status of internal controls in fast moving small medium and micro consumer goods enterprises within the Cape Peninsula. *Mediterranean Journal of Social Sciences, 5*(10), 163

53 Grote & Moss, 2008, cited by Siwangaza, L., Smit, Y., Juan-Pierré, B., & Ukpere, W. I. (2014). The status of internal controls in fast moving small medium and micro consumer goods enterprises within the Cape Peninsula. *Mediterranean Journal of Social Sciences, 5*(10), 163

54 Abor and Adjasi (2007) provide conceptual insights on the application of corporate governance among small and medium enterprises (SMEs) in Ghana. The major finding of the study shows that the application of good corporate governance structure among SMEs in Ghana could help overcome credit constraints and managerial incompetence

55 Drogalas et al., 2005; Karagiorgos et al., 2010, cited by Nyakundi, D. O., Nyamita, M. O., & Tinega, T. M. (2014). Effect of internal control systems on

financial performance of small and medium scale business enterprises in Kisumu City, Kenya. *International Journal of Social Sciences and Entrepreneurship*, *1*(11), 719-734

56   Cheung & Qiang (2002), Stewart & Kent (2006), both cited by Suyono, E., & Hariyanto, E. (2012). Relationship between internal control, internal audit, and organization commitment with good governance: Indonesian case. *China-USA Business Review*, *11*(9).

57   Virginia et al (2009) cited by Suyono, E., & Hariyanto, E. (2012). Relationship between internal control, internal audit, and organization commitment with good governance: Indonesian case. *China-USA Business Review*, *11*(9).

58   Temkin, 2009 cited by Siwangaza, L., Smit, Y., Juan-Pierré, B., & Ukpere, W. I. (2014). The status of internal controls in fast moving small medium and micro consumer goods enterprises within the Cape Peninsula. *Mediterranean Journal of Social Sciences*, *5*(10), 163

59   Parum, Eva. "Does disclosure on corporate governance lead to openness and transparency in how companies are managed?." *Corporate Governance: An International Review* 13, no. 5 (2005): 702-709.

60   Wattanapruttipaisan, T. (2003). Four proposals for improved financing of SME development in ASEAN. *Asian Development Review*, *20*(2), 66-104; Lardon, A., & Deloof, M. (2014). Financial disclosure by SMEs listed on a semi-regulated market: evidence from the Euronext Free Market. *Small Business Economics*, *42*(2), 361-385

61   Parsa, S., Chong, G., & Isimoya, E. (2007). Disclosure of governance information by small and medium-sized companies. *Corporate Governance: The international journal of business in society*, *7*(5), 635-648

62   Abor, J., & Biekpe, N. (2007). Corporate governance, ownership structure and performance of SMEs in Ghana: implications for financing opportunities. *Corporate Governance: The international journal of business in society*, *7*(3), 288-300.

63   Kao and Tan 2002, p. 55 and 157 cited by Wattanapruttipaisan, T. (2003). Four proposals for improved financing of SME development in ASEAN. *Asian Development Review*, *20*(2), 66-104

64   Haniffa & Cooke (20 Haniffa, Roszaini M., and Terry E. Cooke. "The impact of culture and governance on corporate social reporting." *Journal of accounting and public policy* 24, no. 5 (2005): 391-430

65   Wattanapruttipaisan, T. (2003). Four proposals for improved financing of SME development in ASEAN. *Asian Development Review*, *20*(2), 66-104

66   Maher, Maria, and Thomas Andersson. "Corporate governance: effects on firm performance and economic growth." *Available at SSRN 218490* (2000).

67 La Porta, Rafael, Florencio Lopez-de-Silanes, Andrei Shleifer, and Robert Vishny. "Investor protection and corporate valuation." *The journal of finance* 57, no. 3 (2002): 1147-1170.

68 De Holan, Pablo Martin, and Luis Sanz. "Protected by the family? How closely held family firms protect minority shareholders." *Journal of Business Research* 59, no. 3 (2006): 356-359.

69 La Porta, Rafael, Florencio Lopez-de-Silanes, Andrei Shleifer, and Robert Vishny. "Investor protection and corporate valuation." *The journal of finance* 57, no. 3 (2002): 1147-1170

70 De Holan, Pablo Martin, and Luis Sanz. "Protected by the family? How closely held family firms protect minority shareholders." *Journal of Business Research* 59, no. 3 (2006): 356-359. Corbetta, G., & Salvato, C. A. (2004). The board of directors in family firms: one size fits all?. *Family Business Review, 17*(2), 119-134

71 Stanford Research Institute, 1963 cited in Freeman & Reed, 1983, p. 91)

72 Department Trade and Industry, 2001

73 European Commission Recommendation 2003/361/EC of 6 May 2003 concerning the definition of micro, small and medium-sized enterprises, available at http://ec.europa.eu/enterprise/ enterprise_policy/sme_definition/index_en.htm

74 file:///C:/Users/CAlmona/Documents/HOW%20DO%20YOU%20GOVERN%20A%20SMALL%20BUSINESS%20IN%20AFRICA/7%20-%201.%20SMEs%20IN%20ASIA%20AND%20THE%20PACIFIC.pdf

75 Abe, Masato. "SMEs in Asia and the Pacific." *Studies in Trade and Investment* 65 (2009): 1-31.

76 Definition sums up several Nigerian institution definitions of SMEs, i.e. Central Bank, Federal Ministry of Industry, Nigerian Association of Small and Medium Enterprises (NASME)

77 Gibson, Tom, and H. J. Van der Vaart. "Defining SMEs: A less imperfect way of defining small and medium enterprises in developing countries." (2008). https://www.brookings.edu/wp-content/uploads/2016/06/09_development_gibson.pdf

78 Ayyagari, M., Demirguc-Kunt, A., & Maksimovic, V. (2014). Who creates jobs in developing countries?. *Small Business Economics, 43*(1), 75-99.

79 OECD. (2017, May 15). Small, Medium, Strong. Trends in SME Performance and Business Conditions, OECD Publishing, https://doi.org/10.1787/9789264275683-en

80 https://unctad.org/en/PublicationsLibrary/ditccom2019d1_en.pdf

81 Ciampi, Francesco, and Niccolò Gordini. "Small Enterprise Default Prediction Modeling through Artificial Neural Networks: An Empirical Analysis of Italian Small Enterprises." *Journal of Small Business Management* 51, no. 1 (2013): 23-45.

82   Quartey, P., Turkson, E., Abor, J. Y., & Iddrisu, A. M. (2017). Financing the growth of SMEs in Africa: What are the contraints to SME financing within ECOWAS?. *Review of Development Finance*

83   National Bureau of Statistics. Nigeria. 2019

84   The Small and Medium Enterprises Development Agency of Nigeria (SMEDAN) report, 2019

85   Kongolo, Mukole. "Job creation versus job shedding and the role of SMEs in economic development." *African journal of business management* 4, no. 11 (2010): 2288-2295.

86   Ntsika, 2002, cited by Olawale and Garwe, 2010. Obstacles to the growth of new SMEs in South Africa: A principal component analysis approach. African Journal of Business Management Vol. 4(5), pp. 729-738, May 2010. Available online at http://www.academicjournals.org/AJBM

87   http://www.africanreview.com/finance/business/smes-are-growing-kenya-s-economy-3

88   UNIDO report, 1999

89   Li, Yue, and Martin Rama. "Firm dynamics, productivity growth, and job creation in developing countries: The role of micro-and small enterprises." *The World Bank Research Observer* 30, no. 1 (2015): 3-38.

90   Turyakira, Peter, Elmarie Venter, and Elroy Smith. "Corporate social responsibility for SMEs: A proposed hypothesised model." *African Journal of Business Ethics* 6, no. 2 (2012).

91   Headd, B. (2017, September). Small Business Facts: Small Business Job Creation Deconstructed.   https://www.sba.gov/sites/default/files/Job_Creation_fact_sheet_FINAL_0.pdf

92   Sunday, 2011, cited by Tsagem, Muhammad Musa, Norhani Aripin, and Rokiah Ishak. "Impact of working capital management and corporate governance on the profitability of small and medium-sized entities in Nigeria: A proposed model." *International Journal of Science Commerce and Humanities* 2, no. 5 (2014): 53-65.

93   Eniola, Anthony Abiodun, and Harry Ektebang. "SME firms performance in Nigeria: Competitive advantage and its impact." *International Journal of Research Studies in Management* 3, no. 2 (2014): 75-86.

94   Feeney and Riding, 1997, cited by Abor, Joshua, and Peter Quartey. "Issues in SME development in Ghana and South Africa." *International research journal of finance and economics* 39, no. 6 (2010): 215-228.

95   Fischer 1995; Mead and Liedholm 1998, Quartey, Peter, Ebo Turkson, Joshua Y. Abor, and Abdul Malik Iddrisu. "Financing the growth of SMEs in Africa: What are the contraints to SME financing within ECOWAS?." *Review of development finance* 7, no. 1 (2017): 18-28.

96   Aremu & Adeyemi, 2011 cited by Eniola, Anthony Abiodun, and Harry Ektebang. "SME firms performance in Nigeria: Competitive advantage and its

impact." *International Journal of Research Studies in Management* 3, no. 2 (2014): 75-86.

97 Ladzani, Watson M., and Jurie J. Van Vuuren. "Entrepreneurship training for emerging SMEs in South Africa." *Journal of small business management* 40, no. 2 (2002): 154-161.

98 Bowen, G. A. (2009). Document analysis as a qualitative research method. *Qualitative research journal, 9*(2), 27-40

99 FinMark Trust, 2006 cited by Olawale and Garwe, 2010. Obstacles to the growth of new SMEs in South Africa: A principal component analysis approach. African Journal of Business Management Vol. 4(5), pp. 729-738, May 2010. Available online at http://www.academicjournals.org/AJBM

100 Harvard Business Review (HBR) magazine article written by Neil C. Churchill and Virginia L. May 1983. https://hbr.org/1983/05/the-five-stages-of-small-business-growth

101 http://www.internalauditor.me/article/corporate-governance-company-life-cycle/

102 Postma and Zwart (2001), Džafić et al (2011), Wang (2016), Sidik (2012), Moreira (2016) and Quartey et al (2017)

103 Mwarari, M. M., and P. K. Ngugi. "Factors influencing listing of Kenyan SMEs in the securities market for capital raising opportunities." *European journal of management sciences and economics* 1, no. 2 (2013): 99-115.

104 Basil Anthony (2005). "Small and Medium Enterprises (SMEs) in Nigeria: Problems and Prospects", Unpublished PHD Dissertation to St Clement University

105 Abor & Quarty (2010) citing Anheier and Seibel, 1987; Steel and Webster, 1991; Aryeetey et al, 1994; Gockel and Akoena, 2002

106 Stone et al, 1992 cited by Bowen, G. A. (2009). Document analysis as a qualitative research method. *Qualitative research journal, 9*(2), 27-40

107 Bowen, G. A. (2009). Document analysis as a qualitative research method. *Qualitative research journal, 9*(2), 27-40

108 Beck et al, 2005b; Beck and Demirguc-Kunt, 2006; Beck et al, 2006; Ayyagari et al, 2008; Beck et al, 2008a; Ayyagari et al, 2012

109 Fjose, Sveinung, Leo A. Grünfeld, and Chris Green. "SMEs and growth in Sub-Saharan Africa: Identifying SME roles and obstacles to SME growth." *MENON Business Economics Publication* 14 (2010).

110 FinMark Trust Report (2006)

111 Foxcroft, M., E. Wood, J. Kew, M. Herrington, and N. Segal. "Global entrepreneurship monitor: South African executive report." *Graduate School of Business: University of Cape Town* (2002).

112 Barbosa and Moraes (2004), cited by Mahembe, Edmore, and C. Chiumya. "Literature review on small and medium enterprises' access to credit and support

in South Africa." *Underhill Corporate Solutions. National Credit Regulator (NCR): Pretoria, South Africa* (2011).

113 Gunhild, Berg, and Fuchs Michael. "Bank financing of SMEs in five Sub-Saharan African countries: the role of competition, innovation, and the government." *Policy Research Working Paper Series* (2013).

114 Berger and Udell, 1998; Beck et al, 2008b; De la Torre et al, 2010; Beck et al, 2011

115 Dietsch and Petey (2004), cited by Ciampi, Francesco. "Corporate governance characteristics and default prediction modeling for small enterprises. An empirical analysis of Italian firms." *Journal of Business Research* 68, no. 5 (2015): 1012-1025.

116 Slocum, John W., Don Hellriegel, and Susan E. Jackson. *Competency-based management.* Thomson/South-Western, 2008.

117 Martin, G., and H. Staines. "Managerial competencies in small firm. A scoping study." (2008).

118 Orford, John, Eric Wood, C. Fisher, M. Herrington, and N. Segal. "Global entrepreneurship monitor." *South African executive report* (2003).

119 Okten, Cagla, and Una Okonkwo Osili. "Social networks and credit access in Indonesia." *World Development* 32, no. 7 (2004): 1225-1246.

120 Klerk, de GJ & Havenga, JJD (2002). *SME networks and clusters and their impact on economic growth: an exploratory overview of Africa,*www.kmu.unisg. ch/rencontres/RENC2004/Topics/DeKlerk_Havenga_Renc_04_Topic_C.pdf

121 Fatai, Abiodun. "Small and medium scale enterprises in Nigeria: The problems and prospects." *RetrievedJanuary15fromwww. thecje. com/journal/index. php/ economicsjour nal/article/.../8* (2011).

122 Barbosa and Moraes (2004), cited by Mahembe, Edmore, and C. Chiumya. "Literature review on small and medium enterprises' access to credit and support in South Africa." *Underhill Corporate Solutions. National Credit Regulator (NCR): Pretoria, South Africa* (2011).

123 Victoria Onehi and Chris Agabi, 2019. Why small businesses have trouble getting loans. News On A Country January 23, 2019 | Daily Trust. <u>https://www.dailytrust.com.ng/why-small-businesses-have-trouble-getting-loans-2.html</u>

124 Sarbah, Alfred, and W. Xiao. "Corporate governance practices in Ghanaian family businesses: A conceptual framework." *International Journal of Advancements in Research & Technology* 3 (2013): 100-115.

125 Miller, D., Steier, L., & Le Breton-Miller, I. (2003). Lost in time: Intergenerational succession, change, and failure in family business. *Journal of business venturing, 18*(4), 513-531

126 Uhlaner et al. 2007, Afrifa, Godfred Adjappong, and Venancio Tauringana. "Corporate governance and performance of UK listed small and medium enterprises." *Corporate Governance* (2015).

127 Uhlaner, Lorraine, Mike Wright, and Morten Huse. "Private firms and corporate governance: An integrated economic and management perspective." *Small Business Economics* 29, no. 3 (2007): 225-241.

128 https://www.ifc.org/wps/wcm/connect/topics_ext_content/ifc_external_corporate_site/ifc+cg/resources/guidelines_reviews+and+case+studies/sme+governance+guidebook

129 https://www.ifc.org/wps/wcm/connect/bf16179f-e8f1-4261-81ac-2937ee26286f/CG Progression Matrix SME 043019.pdf?MOD=AJPERES&CVID=mGb2MKh

130 Martin Devlin, 2008. Corporate governance in SMEs. https://management.co.nz/article/tabled-governance-smes

131 (Tihanyi, L., Graffin, S., & George, G. (2014). Rethinking governance in management research.

132 Shanmugam, J. K., Haat, M. H. C., & Ali, A. (2012). An exploratory study of internal control and fraud prevention measures in SMEs. *Small, 100*, 18-2.

133 Oseifuah, Emmanuel K., and Agyapong B. Gyekye. "Internal control in small and microenterprises in the Vhembe District, Limpopo Province, South Africa." *European Scientific Journal* 9, no. 4 (2013).

134 Shanmugam, J. K., Haat, M. H. C., & Ali, A. (2012). An exploratory study of internal control and fraud prevention measures in SMEs. *Small, 100*, 18-2.

135 Corbetta, G., & Salvato, C. A. (2004). The board of directors in family firms: one size fits all?. *Family Business Review, 17*(2), 119-134.

136 Holtmann et al (2000, p. 2) cited by Wattanapruttipaisan, T. (2003). Four proposals for improved financing of SME development in ASEAN. *Asian Development Review, 20*(2), 66-104.

137 Wattanapruttipaisan, T. (2003). Four proposals for improved financing of SME development in ASEAN. *Asian Development Review, 20*(2), 66-104.

138 Chu, W. (2009). The influence of family ownership on SME performance: evidence from public firms in Taiwan. *Small Business Economics, 33*(3), 353-373.

139 Shanmugam, J. K., Haat, M. H. C., & Ali, A. (2012). An exploratory study of internal control and fraud prevention measures in SMEs. *Small, 100*, 18-2.

140 Luyolo et al. 2014, cited by Aladejebi, Olufemi Adepoju. "Strategies for Improving Internal Control in Small and Medium Enterprises in Nigeria." (2017).),

141 Oseifuah, E. K., & Gyekye, A. B. (2013). Internal control in small and microenterprises in the Vhembe District, Limpopo Province, South Africa. *European Scientific Journal, ESJ, 9*(4)

142 Jiang, L., & Li, X. (2010). Discussions on the Improvement of the Internal Control in SMEs. *International Journal of Business and Management, 5*(9), 214.

143 Shanmugam, J. K., Haat, M. H. C., & Ali, A. (2012). An exploratory study of internal control and fraud prevention measures in SMEs. *Small, 100*, 18-2.

144 Jiang, L., & Li, X. (2010). Discussions on the Improvement of the Internal Control in SMEs. *International Journal of Business and Management, 5*(9), 214.

145 https://www.accaglobal.com/content/dam/acca/global/PDF-technical/small-business/ea-governance-for-all.pdf

146 www.waspbarcode.com › small-business-report

147 https://www.tradegecko.com/hubfs/eBooks/TradeGecko_eBook_whitepaper_2018-2019_state_of_small_business_global_report.pdf?hsLang=en-us

148 https://www.guidantfinancial.com/2019-small-business-trends/

149 Aremu, Mukaila Ayanda, and Sidikat Laraba Adeyemi. "Small and medium scale enterprises as a survival strategy for employment generation in Nigeria." *Journal of sustainable development* 4, no. 1 (2011): 200.

150 Amankwah-Amoah, Joseph, Nathaniel Boso, and Yaw A. Debrah. "Africa rising in an emerging world: an international marketing perspective." *International Marketing Review* (2018).

151 Gbandi, E. C., and G. Amissah. "Financing options for small and medium enterprises (SMEs) in Nigeria." *European scientific journal* 10, no. 1 (2014).

152 Aryeetey, Ernest, and William Baah-Boateng. *Understanding Ghana's growth success story and job creation challenges.* No. 2015/140. WIDER Working Paper, 2015

153 Wattanapruttipaisan, T. (2003). Four proposals for improved financing of SME development in ASEAN. *Asian Development Review, 20*(2), 66-104

154 Calice, Pietro, Victor M. Chando, and Sofiane Sekioua. "Bank financing to small and medium enterprises in East Africa: findings of a survey in Kenya, Tanzania, Uganda and Zambia." (2012).

155 OECD principles, 2004

156 Petra, K. (2013) Stakeholder engagement: a practical guide. Accessed from https://www.theguardian.com/sustainable-business/stakeholder-engagement-practical guide

157 The International Integrated Reporting Council. The International Integrated Reporting Framework available at https://integratedreporting.org/wp-content/uploads/2015/03/13-12-08-THE-INTERNATIONAL-IR-FRAMEWORK-2-1.pdf

158 https://www.forumforthefuture.org/the-five-capitals

159 Davidsson, P. and Honig, B (2003). 'The role of social and human capital among nascent entrepreneurs', J. of business venturing, 18 (3), pp. 301-331.

160 Biggs, Tyler, and Manju Kedia Shah. *African small and medium enterprises, networks, and manufacturing performance.* The World Bank, 2006.

161 https://www.efaa.com/cms/upload/efaa_files/pdf/Publications/Articles/IRforSMEs_EFAA.pdf

162 https://www.ifac.org/system/files/publications/files/Creating-Value-for-SMEs-through-Integrated-Thinking.pdf

163 Gabrielsson, Jonas, and Morten Huse. "Outside directors in SME boards: a call for theoretical reflections." *Corporate Board: role, duties and composition* 1, no. 1 (2005): 28-37.

164 https://en.wikipedia.org/wiki/Family_business

165 ***Source:*** *Nancy Upton and William Petty, "Venture Capital Investment in Family Business," Venture Capital, 2000, Vol. 2, No. 1, pp. 27-39*

166 http://venturesafrica.com/the-african-family-owned-business-a-partner-for-private-equity/

167 Gallo M.A., Kenyon-Rouvinez D. (2005) The Importance of Family and Business Governance. In: Family Business. A Family Business Publication. Palgrave Macmillan, London. pp 45-57

168 **Grant Gordon and Nigel Nicholson. *Family Wars. Classic conflicts in family business and how to live with them***

169 Miller et al, 2003 citing Davis and Harveston 1998, p. 32; Handler, 1990, 1992; Sonnenfeld, 1988, p. 238; Ward, 1997, p. xvi

170 Chu, W. (2009). The influence of family ownership on SME performance: evidence from public firms in Taiwan. *Small Business Economics*, *33*(3), 353-373.

171 https://www.ifc.org/wps/wcm/connect/topics_ext_content/ifc_external_corporate_site/ifc+cg/resources/guidelines_reviews+and+case+studies/ifc+family+business+governance+handbook